ESCAPE
IN
IRAQ

The Thomas Hamill Story

by Thomas Hamill & Paul T. Brown
Edited by Jay Langston

Stoeger Publishing Company, Accokeek, Maryland

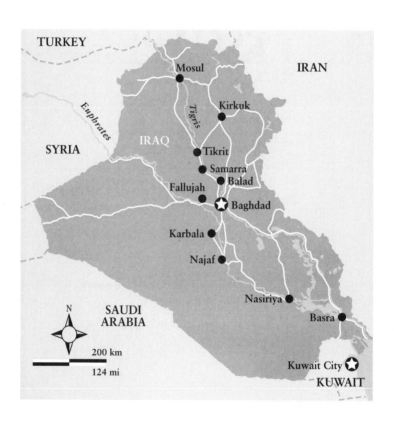

ESCAPE IN IRAQ

The Thomas Hamill Story

by Thomas Hamill & Paul T. Brown

Edited by Jay Langston

Stoeger Publishing.
Great Outdoor Books & More Since 1924

STOEGER PUBLISHING COMPANY
is a division of Benelli U.S.A.

Benelli U.S.A.
Vice President and General Manager:
  Stephen Otway
*Vice President of Marketing and
Communications:* Stephen McKelvain

Stoeger Publishing Company
President: Jeffrey Reh
Publisher & Editor: Jay Langston
Managing Editor: Harris J. Andrews
Design & Production Director:
  Cynthia T. Richardson
Photography Director: Alex Bowers
Imaging Specialist: William Graves
National Sales Manager: Jennifer Thomas
Special Accounts Manager: Julie Brownlee
Publishing Assistants: Tina Talmadge,
  Shannon McWilliams
Proofreader: Celia Beattie

Published in cooperation with
True Exposures Publishing, Inc.
President: Paul T. Brown
Publishing Assistants: Jessica Brown,
Mark A. Brown, Terry Mullen,
Janet Watkins

Published by Stoeger Publishing Company
17603 Indian Head Highway, Suite 200
Accokeek, Maryland 20607

BK0425
ISBN: 0-88317-314-X
Library of Congress Control Number:
2004110706

Manufactured in the United States of
America. Distributed to the book trade
and to the sporting goods trade by:
Stoeger Industries
17603 Indian Head Highway, Suite 200
Accokeek, Maryland 20607
301-283-6300   Fax: 301-283-6986
www.stoegerpublishing.com

Photography Credits:
Paul T. Brown;
vii, 23, 93, 95, 145, 161, 281, 282, 283, 284
Andrew Innerarity/Houston Chronicle; xi, 35
Courtesy Mark Lee; 25
Courtesy of the Goodrich family; 54
Australian Broadcasting Corporation; 55, 65
Illustration by Reggie McLeroy; 74
DOD/Private 2nd Class Brandi Marshall,
  U.S. Army; 75
Courtesy U.S. Army/Spec. Jacob A. McDonald; 132
Courtesy U.S. Army/Sgt. 1st Class Joe Belcher; 133
Courtesy U.S. Army/Staff Sgt. Charles B. Johnson;
  157
Courtesy U.S. Army/Pfc. James Matise; 175
Alex Bowers; 191
Courtesy U.S. Air Force/Tech. Sgt. Justin D. Pyle;
  209
Courtesy U.S. Army/ Pfc. Blanka Stratford; 215
AP/U.S. Army; 240, 241
DOD/Mr. Harald Risch, U.S. Army; 270
Paul Brown Jr.; 274

*This book is dedicated to
my grandmother, Vera Hamill,
whose love, support, and example of faith
shaped my life, and in loving memory of
my grandfather, Carter Hamill.*

ACKNOWLEDGMENTS

I would like to thank the U.S. Military leadership and personnel in all regions of the world for defending our freedom and for their service to this great country.

My gratitude goes out to the Army Reserve 724th Transportation Company for their courage under fire on April 9, 2004, and to the 2nd Battalion, 108th Infantry New York National Guard for being in the right place at the right time.

I also wish to express my thanks to KBR and their family support group, close friends, and family for their encouragement during my captivity in Iraq. I also would like to recognize the thousands of civilian contractors who support the military worldwide.

I am grateful to the community of Macon, Mississippi, for their support of my family throughout our ordeal. And a special thanks to all of those who prayed for us during our time of need.

Kellie and I appreciate Wallace and Georgia Green for being the rock that held us all together.

May God bless you and your families.

Equipped with flak vest and helmet, Thomas Hamill prepares for convoy duty in Iraq.

PREFACE

Like most Americans, I was captivated by the story of a fellow citizen taken hostage in Iraq on April 9, 2004, during an attack on his convoy. It hit close to home when the wounded man, sitting next to a masked gunman in the backseat of a car, stated his name to a reporter on the scene, "Hamill. Thomas." Then the news anchor said he was from Macon, Mississippi, which made it personal. An unspoken bond connects those of us who call the Magnolia State home. My interest in the story grew each day to near obsession.

My impressions of Mr. Hamill after he concluded his statement to the reporter with "That's all I'm going to say" was that he was fuming mad, tough as nails, and had a resolve that would be difficult for his captors to conquer. I knew those terrorists were going to have a difficult time taming that country boy. Still, I feared for his life.

Every day of his captivity I searched the newspaper and flipped from one local television station to the next hunting for any news of Mr. Hamill's fate. Then, four days into his captivity, his wife, Kellie, appeared briefly on television. She looked worn and tired, but, even in those most perplexing circumstances she displayed the same doggedness her husband had revealed a few days earlier.

As one day faded into the next, not only did I fear the worst, I expected it. I was afraid that with each passing day there was less likelihood he'd be found alive. When news came that he had escaped I was stunned and elated. Then I thought back to my first impression of the man in the backseat of that car showing his anger and defiance and I simply thought, I should've known he'd get away. I should've had more faith.

The humility of Mr. Hamill's words and deeds in the days after his escape compelled me to dig deeper. Speaking with Mr. Hamill and his wife convinced me that I should get involved. I felt led to help share their compelling story. With their consent, we set a time to meet.

The meager 107 miles between my home and the Hamill's practically makes us neighbors. Driving up Highway 25 through the picturesque rolling hills of rural east-central Mississippi for my first meeting with Thomas Hamill, I pondered the unknown. I felt honored to be considered to assist the Hamills in writing a book. I was excited about meeting someone whom I considered an American hero. At the same time, I puzzled that I might find a man so traumatized by his ordeal that he would conceal the details of his experience. Would fear block out his memories? Had the events of the past month driven a wedge between Mr. Hamill and his family? Time spent with the Hamills answered all of my questions with a single, resounding, "NO."

What I discovered was a man of candor, courage, faith, resilience, and humility. I found a man closer to his God and family than he was before all of this happened. The first thing Tommy Hamill told me was, "This story is not about me, it is about the message." His expression was revealing. True to my first impression, he meant what he said and said what he meant. "I don't consider myself to be a hero," he reminded me, "I'm just an ordinary man."

After brokering an agreement between Tommy and Stoeger Publishing to publish this book, I spent days and weeks recording his life's story. I learned what molded a man to withstand 24 days of captivity by a band of thugs.

He definitely was candid. Tommy was open and truthful about his time spent as a hostage. He answered all of my questions with a candor that revealed details of his experience that had not been exposed previously. Tommy assured me, "I am not going to hold back."

When cast into dire straights, nearly all of us pray akin to James Stewart's character George Bailey in the 1947 motion picture, *It's A Wonderful Life*. George, at the end of his rope, sat at the bar in Martini's praying frantically for God to show him the way out of certain financial ruin. Not Tommy. In the face of probable death, he calmly "talked" to God, turning a seemingly hopeless situation completely over to Him, and then had the faith, the trust, and the confidence God would carry out His will.

The impact that Tommy and his story has had, and continues to have, on listeners is amazing. I sat in a country church in Oktibbeha County, Mississippi, observing Tommy address a National Guard unit that was preparing to deploy to Iraq. Uplifted by his powerful story, Tommy's words touched everybody in the crowded sanctuary in a special way.

One day, while Tommy and I were wrapping up a long day of interviewing at his house, a loud knock on the back door interrupted our conversation. Tommy opened the door and there stood two bewildered and awestruck men. They introduced themselves and explained that they had driven two days from a Midwestern state for the off chance of meeting Tommy. The men did not call in advance. They had no idea Tommy would be home or would even meet them. As Tommy talked with the men I whispered to Kellie, "Does this happen often?" She merely shrugged her shoulders and answered, "Yeah, it's happened several times." Since meeting Tommy, I have witnessed what great lengths people will go to reach out, to "touch the stone," to connect with that unseen force that helps them cope with life's struggles.

Knowing the Hamill family has enriched my life. I am privileged to now call them friends. I hope *Escape in Iraq: The Thomas Hamill Story* will inspire you to seek help with life's woes and rejoice in its glories with a renewed perspective.

— Paul T. Brown

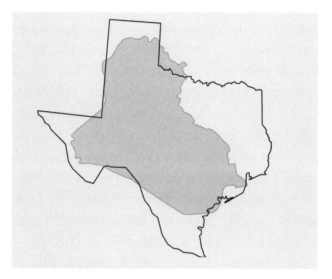

*The country of Iraq (shaded) is somewhat smaller
than the state of Texas.*

Baghdad

ESCAPE
IN
IRAQ

The Thomas Hamill Story

by Thomas Hamill & Paul T. Brown
Edited by Jay Langston

INTRODUCTION

On March 19, 2003, President George W. Bush made an announcement to the nation.

"My fellow citizens, at this hour, American and coalition forces are in the early stages of military operations to disarm Iraq, to free its people and to defend the world from grave danger.

On my orders, coalition forces have begun striking selected targets of military importance to undermine Saddam Hussein's ability to wage war. These are opening stages of what will be a broad and concerted campaign...

To all the men and women of the United States Armed Forces now in the Middle East, the peace of a troubled world and the hopes of an oppressed people now depend on you. That trust is well placed.

May God bless our country and all who defend her."

On the following day, American and coalition ground forces began Operation Iraqi Freedom striking into Iraq across the border from Kuwait. Within a day, Coalition forces had crossed the Euphrates River, and, after heavy fighting against Republican Guard and other Iraqi forces at Nasiriya, Najaf, Karbala, and Kut, American forces entered Baghdad on April 5. Two days later, British troops captured the southern port city of Basra and by the 9th Saddam Hussein's governmental authority had collapsed. In the north, Kurdish fighters and American Special Forces captured the cities of Kirkuk and Mosul by April 11, and Tikrit, Saddam Hussein's hometown, fell without opposition four days later. Shortly afterward, the Pentagon announced that "major combat engagements" had ended.

Within a month, however, it became obvious that numerous guerrilla organizations were coalescing in various regions of Iraq, all dedicated to opposing the presence of Coalition forces and preparing themselves for an ultimate power struggle should U.S. forces withdraw. In central Iraq, former supporters of the Saddam regime, primarily of Sunni origin, merged with local tribal groups and religious fundamentalists. In many cases they may have been organized by survivors of the Fedayeen Saddam, a shadowy paramilitary organization created and armed by Saddam Hussein shortly before the war. In the predominately Shi'a south, followers of cleric Muqtada al-Sadr organized the so-called Mahdi Army militia, drawing strength from unemployed young men in Shi'a communities and in the slums of Baghdad's Sadr

City. There has been strong indication that various insurgent groups have received support from foreign Islamic fundamentalist "volunteers."

As attacks on Coalition forces increased in number and intensity, private contractors providing logistical support for American forces found themselves on the front lines. When U.S. forces began to establish bases in Iraq, the largest private corporation providing logistical support — engineers, cooks, logistics experts, and transportation personnel — was KBR, (Kellogg Brown & Root), operating under the U.S. Army's Logistics Civil Augmentation Program. Military contractors since World War II, KBR's Government Operations branch has successfully housed, fed, and maintained American fighting forces in several remote and politically dangerous regions including Somalia and Afghanistan. Among KBR's most vital services is the transportation of all the sinews of war: food, individual equipment, fuel, construction materials, medical supplies, and repair parts to name but a few, every ton of which has to be hauled by truck from Kuwait or in-country depots to military bases throughout Iraq.

For the KBR truckers, the war began in May 2003. Unwilling to face American firepower, Iraqi guerrilla cells turned their attention to the American supply convoys. Roadside bombs, improvised from discarded Iraqi artillery shells and bombs — detonated by remote control — and hit-and-run ambush with rocket-propelled grenades and automatic weapons fire increasingly became hazards of the road. In the early morning of August 5,

2003, a U.S. mail convoy of three heavily loaded trucks left the Baghdad Airport headed north. Near Tikrit, a bomb detonated under one of the trucks. The driver, Fred Bryant Jr., was rushed to a military field hospital, but died en route. Bryant was KBR's first combat casualty in Iraq's road war. There would be many more. It was onto these dangerous highways that Thomas Hamill, a 43-year-old farmer and truck driver from Mississippi, ventured in the fall of 2003.

It all goes back to my childhood. From the time I was old enough to think about it I was convinced that when I got old enough I would automatically go into the service and almost certainly go to war somewhere. My friends and I grew up admiring American heroes like Sergeant Alvin York in World War I and the great leaders of World War II, men like Patton, Marshall, Eisenhower, as well as fighting soldiers like Audi Murphy. Patriotism was something you absorbed, kind of like breathing; it didn't need a lot of conscious effort.

By the time I was getting toward high-school age, the war in Vietnam had been going on for years, and it looked like it was never going to end. I don't know whether it was a feeling of patriotism or the fact that I had an uncle serving in Vietnam, but I understood at a pretty young age that our people were over there sacrificing themselves for our safety and freedom. I also realized that a lot of people back home just didn't care or pay much attention to what was going on in Southeast Asia. I used to watch Dan Rather and the other correspondents on the television news, and they always brought up body counts; that's what you would hear more than anything else. I came to accept that, in the future, when I got out of school, I would join the military and would be sent over there to fight. That's the way I had it figured — it was simply what was going to happen.

Sports were another fact of life. When I was 15, in the ninth grade, I desperately wanted to play football. Even though I was fairly small, I still wanted to get out there with the big guys. Only two of us 15-year-olds tried out that year, and I played linebacker and split end at 130 pounds.

I had been playing for about a year when I had my first seizure. Our family doctor referred me to Dr. Glen Warren, a neurosurgeon in Jackson, Mississippi. Dr. Warren warned me not to play any sports where I would have the chance of bumping my head. He started me on seizure medication. In football you are definitely going to get your head jarred. I still played that year, and began playing the next year. I really had to think hard about my situation. Football meant a lot to me, but I had read that some people had seizures as frequently as 30 minutes. I kept thinking, I don't want to be like that and ruin my life forever.

One day, in my junior year, a Marine recruiter showed up at school. He told us that we could sign up for a pre-enlistment and get all our tests and other preliminaries out of the way. That way, when we graduated in two years, we could go right on to boot camp. Even though the war in Vietnam had ended, I still wanted to serve my country. Several of us signed up and got our paperwork and testing done. I thought, all I had to do was graduate from high school and I could join the Marines. I finally decided that I had to tell the recruiters about my seizures. I didn't know what kind of trouble it might cause if I tried to keep it a secret. I'd have had to try and hide my medication to prevent seizures in boot camp and hope no one found out. I didn't think I could pull it off, so I told my recruiter. He was sympathetic but said that the Marines couldn't take me. I was really upset. First I was locked out of playing football, and then I couldn't join the service. Both of my youthful goals had been torn from my grasp.

My family belonged to the Methodist Church, but like many young people, I didn't know much about it. I still believed in God through all this. I still believed that Jesus died for our sins, but I never got down on my knees to pray the sinner's prayer. I never said, "God, I am a sinner. Will you forgive me for my sins. I am going to turn my whole life over to God and Jesus. I am going to live and follow you." I just didn't feel like I was worthy enough. But God has shown me that we are all worthy; all we have to do is call upon his name regardless of what we have done. In my life I've learned a lot the hard way, and sometimes when you learn that way and survive, you won't go back and do it again. At the time, though, I just thought that as long as I believed in God, I'd have plenty of time to get down on my knees and beg for his grace, but now I realize that sometimes tomorrow may not come. The next minute may not come. If you haven't gotten right with God it is too late.

I have worked hard ever since I can remember. Growing up on a farm I always had chores. One of my jobs when I was little was to feed all of the calves. And I helped milk cows when I couldn't even see over them. I also recall pushing a lawn mower when I had to reach up to grab the handlebars. In grade school I spent my summers cutting grass in town while my friends were out having fun. Most people don't think about it, but farming is one of the world's most dangerous occupations. Kids — and adults for that matter — who work on small farms regularly do things that would probably be covered by all sorts of safety rules in any other business. It's always a scramble to make a living and keep a farm going. Even at a young age you've got to work around big domestic animals and dangerous pieces of farm machinery.

I think I've always had diesel smoke in my blood. I wanted to be able to drive a truck for as long as I can remember. When I was little, Daddy worked for Dairymen, Inc., and Noxubee Milk Producers driving supply trucks and hauling milk for our local milk plant. I used to ride down to work with him standing up on the floorboard and could barely see over the dash. Every time he would get out to make a pickup I jumped over behind the steering wheel. That old truck just amazed me. The dashboard was overwhelming, and it had a gauge for everything, just like an airplane. The very thought of having to puzzle out the purpose of all those mysterious buttons, switches, and dials was scary.

I also wanted to drive a tractor, but Daddy didn't want

9

me on a tractor at a young age. He finally let me drive when I was about ten or eleven. We had a very small, old tractor with a small, six-foot disk to plow our hay fields. We planted brown-top millet or Sudan grass for hay. All of our hay was put up in square bales, and my first job on the tractor was hauling bales from the field to the barn. The next year, Daddy let me start running the tractor with farm implements.

I learned to drive a truck when I was a teenager. I started out driving our pickup truck in the hay fields. It was a three-speed stick on-the-column model, and I could barely reach the clutch pedal. One of my plans was to learn truck driving in the military. I needed experience, and there weren't any truck-driving schools around. Unless you had experience no one would hire you. Since my plans to join the Marines had been frustrated, I was determined to work my way up, learning to drive a truck little by little. I had several driving jobs over the years and every time I made a change, I gained a little more experience and moved up a little higher.

In 1985 I went to work for Richard Canull who owned Canull Trucking Company in Brooksville, Mississippi, and by 1990 I wanted to buy my own truck. I learned about the trucking business, keeping up with fuel, other expenses, and freight rates. I was convinced I could succeed if I could just get someone to finance a truck. Unfortunately I couldn't get anyone — the banks especially — to even talk to me about a loan for a truck. I didn't know what to do so I talked to Mr. Canull and explained my problem. He said he'd go have a talk with his banker. He persuaded the loan officer at the bank to make the loan and he put up half of a CD as collateral. Thanks to Mr. Canull I bought my first used truck. I learned how to repair trucks while working for Canull Trucking Company, too, so I could do most of the maintenance work to avoid costly shop bills. I kept that truck for a few years before buying a second truck that I drove until 1997.

I met Kellie on September 10, 1986, in the middle of a run from California to Alexandria, Louisiana. I made a stopover in Amarillo, Texas, at a Truck Stops of America to take a shower and spend the night. The company I was driving for at the time was a big account for the truck stop and one of the perks was our drivers got free showers whether we bought fuel or not.

I went inside to get my shower, but the lady at the desk said I had to have a coupon or pay for the shower. I proceeded to tell her that I worked for a company that got free showers for their drivers. She was adamant about me not getting a free shower and insisted I pay. I got upset. She got on the phone with the fuel desk and told me I'd have to walk over there to get a shower coupon. She said if the lady at the fuel desk would give me a coupon she'd allow me to take a shower.

I went to the fuel desk with an attitude. I noticed the lady's name was Kellie as I proceeded to chew her out. She broke my tirade by throwing a stapler at me.

The next morning I felt guilty about how I had behaved,

so I went back and apologized to Kellie and asked her to join me for breakfast. Our relationship grew over the next 10 months and we were married on July 9, 1987.

In 1994 I bought our farm from my dad and uncle. I worked as an independent trucker, and had to run the farm as well. I'd hit the road on a job, be gone all week, and have to service the truck when I returned. I had a hired hand to milk the cows when I was gone. Daddy always helped me cut hay. If we needed hay he would cut it on a Thursday and bale it on Saturday when I got off the road. I had a small herd and business was good, so I felt confident enough to buy a few more cows.

Milk prices went up and down, but as long as prices were up, we made a good income. I wanted to increase the size of my herd and bought 35 more milk cows from a farmer in our county who was in the process of selling out. Eventually we owned nearly 100 head of cattle. We still had an old-style barn and were milking 100 cows a day with antiquated milking machines. It took three of us — including my nearly seventy-year-old father — more than 10 hours per day just to get the milking done. I had to do something. We were killing ourselves.

I heard that a dairy farm down in southern Mississippi was shutting down, and I knew I needed better equipment. I borrowed the money to buy the farmer's milking machines so I could get my own operation running smoother. The newer milking machines could milk 100 cows in ninety minutes. I told Kellie that if we could have one more good year maybe we could get on our feet. It didn't work out that way. Soon after I spent the money to handle more milking capacity, milk prices started dropping.

When I purchased the newer equipment, milk was $19 per hundred pounds. My break-even price was set at $13 per hundred pounds of milk. Anything less and business would go in the red. Prices stayed low for more than a year. Even worse, I didn't have a lot of usable grazing land on the farm and had to buy expensive commercial feed to get the amount of milk I needed. I was forced to work more days driving a truck just to pay our $7,000 to $8,000 per month feed bill. I also had to swap my days around so I could be home to bale hay. We were putting up 1,500 to 1,600 rolls a year. To keep up with bills, I pushed myself harder.

I wasn't getting any rest. I hauled milk in the truck all night long, and when I got home at sunrise I had to help Daddy cut and bale hay. Two days of that would wear me out completely. One day, in the spring of 2002, between Highway 45 and Aberdeen on Route 8, I collapsed. I had one more barn's milk to pick up that day, and I laid my head down for a few minutes on the steering wheel to sleep. I must have dozed for about thirty minutes. After the milk was pumped into my tanker, I started down the road without being fully awake. I must have fallen back asleep and dropped off on the shoulder of the road. When I woke up I jerked the truck back onto the road. I tried to slow down, braking carefully to keep from jackknifing. Suddenly I heard a loud bang, and the truck flipped over. Everything seemed to happen in slow motion. I could hear metal crunching and saw sparks flying through the cab. The roof started caving in, and asphalt flew in through the smashed front window like a sandblaster. I had just enough time to think. *This is going to be it; I am going to die.* I fell onto the roof and all of a sudden everything was calm.

I found myself in the rear of the cab. When I leaned back I fell out on the ground through the back window. The glass had popped out. I realized if I had worn my seat belt it would have killed me. The impact had thrown me across the seat and I was pushed between the seats and the back glass. Amazingly, I was okay. I got up and looked around to make sure the truck was out of the road.

The remains of Thomas Hamill's milk truck in a wrecking yard near Macon, Mississippi. The crash nearly cost Tommy his life.

The following year things got worse. The farm was getting run down, and I was working myself to death just trying to break even. I didn't want to quit. I didn't want to give up on my farm even if it meant working my fingers to a nub. One day I ran into a truck driver who had leased his rig to the same company that I contracted for about five years earlier. He remembered that I had a farm. I told him I was thinking about making some kind of change — maybe buy another truck and drive full time — I wasn't sure what. He mentioned that there was a guy he knew who had stored his truck and was driving for a company called KBR in Iraq. According to my acquaintance he was making good money over there.

The next day I drove up north of Kosciusko, Mississippi, to pick up milk on one of the farms on my routes. I mentioned driving in Iraq to the farmer and he told me that one of his neighbors, Kenneth Horne, was also working over there. I decided to call his wife. I was excited about the idea of driving overseas.

A few days later I called Kenneth's wife and asked her all about what he was doing over in Iraq and what kind of money he was making. She said, "Well, why don't you just call Kenny?" I was a little startled and asked if he was coming home soon. She said that he was still in Iraq but had a cell phone. I called and he told me what he was doing and, at that time, contract truckers were only going a little ways into Iraq, offloading, and going back to Kuwait. Until the situation was secure, he said, the military drivers took supplies the rest of the way to the forward bases and depots. Kenneth did tell me that there was some danger. One KBR driver had already been killed.

Up until that time I hadn't thought much about the war in Iraq. I knew about the fighting from the news but I hadn't known about civilians working over there. If I went I'd be doing the same thing that regular military transportation units did. That seemed to be a pretty good deal to me. I already knew how to drive a truck, and I needed the money. KBR would pay me $16 to $18 per hour for a yearlong contract that would be worth about $75,000, all of which would be tax-free as long as I remained in Iraq for the full term of my contract. Not only that, but I would finally have a chance to do something for my country, to give back something to those soldiers in the past who had served their country so I could enjoy freedom. I wanted to be able to say that I went and did my part.

Soon after, I told Kellie what I had on my mind; I was determined to go. I was honest with her about the dangers involved. We had seen the violence on TV and I wanted her to be aware of the risk. If something bad happened to me I didn't want it to come as a surprise to Kellie. There was another problem, however, money was tight, and we had to make our monthly payments of $1,600 on a cattle and milking-equipment loan plus a $500 land payment. I knew that while KBR would pick up all of the costs of my attending a seven-day orientation class in Houston, contract employees only got paid within five to seven days of the last Saturday of the month. This meant that Kellie and I would be a whole month without income. To make ends meet, I sold all of my cattle on the 18th of August.

I flew down to Houston on the 25th of August to start my KBR orientation. By the 3rd of September, I had completed my background check and physical and everything was set. I'd be on the next flight to Iraq when they called my name. Three weeks passed. The KBR officials said that they were waiting for all of the equipment to be put in place.

Finally, KBR started paying us about $200 a week. It helped out a little for household expenses, but I was painfully aware that it would be another month before I got a full paycheck. I didn't know whether we would be able to make our $1,600 monthly payment. By the last week in September, I made up my mind that if they didn't call my name within a day or so that I was going to tell them I had to go home. I just couldn't go another month without a check. Thankfully, they called me the next day, and I flew out on the 28th.

KBR flew us into Kuwait where we were given a second round of training courses. They had us attend defensive-driving courses where we discussed things such as convoy formations, how to spot explosive devices, booby traps, and how to recognize and avoid suspicious automobiles. We watched videos about what we could expect once our convoys entered Iraq. All of the contractor's trucks were concentrated at a place called Truckville, a part of Camp Arifjan, south of Kuwait City. Like the other U.S. Military bases in Kuwait, it was a huge square patch of desert with a 10-foot earthen berm bulldozed to form a perimeter. They are called *kabals*, or fortresses, in Arabic.

I spent a couple of days in Truckville. Everyone was assigned a brand-new Mercedes truck and fully loaded trailer. I think there were seven or eight of us who were going to form our convoy. KBR started our mission with a meeting to issue safety and task instructions. The convoy commander discussed hazard identification and talked about dangers we might encounter. We ran final checks on our trucks and equipment and made sure all of the drivers were prepared. We were told that we would follow another convoy into Iraq and when we got to our destination, a depot somewhere, we were to unload. After that, none of us knew what to expect. On the same day, another convoy that was coming down from north of Baghdad along our route was attacked and one of the trailers was struck by a rocket propelled grenade. The driver was lucky the RPG didn't explode.

We were stationed at Cedar II, a base about 20 miles from Nasiriya in southern Iraq for three months, running back and forth from Cedar II to Camp Anaconda north of Baghdad in the town of Balad. We were working hard, about sixteen or seventeen hours a day and drove for 45 days straight before we got our first half-day off. At that time I wasn't particularly worried about getting shot at. I was more concerned about running into the back of the truck in front of me. We had some pretty bad wrecks when a driver lost his concentration and smashed into the truck ahead when it braked. Most of the accidents were caused by third country nationals, hired by KBR from Pakistan, India, and a score of other places. A lot of those guys drove like maniacs.

I was more worried about some of my fellow drivers than any roadside or terrorist ambush. It was the trucks with the label "Danger — Flammable" on the back that I kept an eye on. The fact was you had to have good driving skills because the road we traveled on was slick when it rained. It was worse than ice. Most of the roads were asphalt and concrete with stretches of sand and dirt. When I was driving a milk truck I spent plenty of time running on gravel and dirt roads, but a lot of the guys in our convoys didn't have my experience.

A lot of the instincts and skills that I had developed during years of driving a truck on Mississippi back roads helped me in Iraq. Most of my fellow truckers were over-the-road drivers who had never been on a dirt road. That's one of the reasons I was offered the job of convoy commander. At first I didn't want the job because I felt my skills were more useful in driving a truck. But I soon realized that they needed someone with experience so I agreed to take the job. I became a transportation coordinator in the last week of November, and about a week later they made me assistant convoy commander. Eventually, I was appointed convoy commander for a couple of missions.

One evening in February someone came and told me I had an emergency message to call home. I was terrified that somebody had been hurt or that a family member had died. I never thought that the emergency involved Kellie. I got her on the phone and she was crying. I got her to calm down, and she said something about heart surgery. She explained that she had to have emergency heart surgery. The doctors had discovered that she needed an aortic valve replacement. It was a life-threatening situation. She had to have surgery immediately. I hung up the phone and sat down. I don't cry much, but at that moment all I could do was sit there and cry. I was terrified for Kellie and asked God why I had been sent all the way to Iraq just to face this situation.

Kellie needed to have surgery within a week, and I needed to get home fast. With the help of the Red Cross, I could get an emergency flight on a military transport plane from the PAX Terminal — the military personnel terminal at Camp Anaconda in Balad — but as a civilian, there was a good chance someone might bump me off. I talked to the people at KBR, and they suggested I ask the Red Cross to send an emergency message to make sure I got a flight and didn't get bumped.

It normally takes a couple of days to process out of Iraq. I rushed around trying to figure out where I needed to go, trying to get everything checked in and signed off. I had to make certain all equipment, like my radio, was turned in. I got it done within two hours that morning. I just made it to the PAX Terminal in time to catch my flight. But I didn't get out that day.

I finally made it onto the C-130 transportation aircraft on February 7th and flew to Kuwait, then boarded a KLM Royal Dutch Airlines jet and flew to Amsterdam. From Amsterdam I took a Delta jet to Atlanta, then changed planes and flew into Jackson, Mississippi. I made it in time to meet Kellie and her dad at the hospital. I still didn't know how serious Kellie's medical condition was. Greg Duncan, our new pastor, whom I hadn't met before I left for Iraq, came over to the hospital. They took Kellie away for some pre-surgery testing and I sat and talked with Brother Greg for a while. After testing, the surgeon decided to go ahead with the operation. While talking with the surgeon later, he told me that he had also discovered and repaired an aortic aneurysm. The surgery went well, and five days later she was out of the hospital.

I then had a serious decision to make. I was committed to go back to Iraq, but I was also needed at home. I felt I had to go back to fulfill my contract and serve my country. I talked it over with Kellie, telling her that all of our friends and everybody at the church were all willing to pitch in. They would do anything they could to help us. I explained that I felt I had to go back. Ominously, while we discussed our immediate future, the news on the hospital room television was full of stories of kidnapped foreign journalists, and it seemed that the fighting was getting worse.

I got back to Iraq on March 7th. I expected to be back home by the first of October and would be gone for almost six months. We were on rotation at that point, driving a couple of days and spending the next few days working at Camp Anaconda.

We were then stationed at Camp Anaconda, a base built on an Iraqi military airfield near the town of Balad, 40 miles north of Baghdad. Camp Anaconda housed about

17,000 men and had a perimeter measuring 12½ miles.

By the time I got to Camp Anaconda, there had been some fighting in the area. American patrols around Balad had been ambushed by guerrillas armed with AK-47 assault rifles, rocket-propelled grenades, and heavy machine guns. There had been mortar attacks on the camp itself.

As convoy commander, I went out on several missions to different camps. On April 7th we had an uneventful run to Camp Ridgeway. We offloaded and returned to Camp Anaconda on the 8th. We were told that there would be two convoys going out the next day, April 9th. They would be long routes and we would be split up into two convoys, with 17 or 18 trucks in each. We uploaded and parked the trucks, ate, and I settled into my hooch for the night.

Tommy checks on a herd of dairy cows.

*Thomas, Tori, and Kellie pose with Tommy at the
Jackson International Airport as he heads for Houston
to begin his training with KBR.*

Thomas Hamill stands next to a line of new Mercedes tankers used by KBR to transport fuel in Iraq.

CHAPTER 1

**GOOD FRIDAY,
APRIL 9, 2004
IRAQ**

IRAQ'S FIRST
ANNIVERSARY OF
FREEDOM

A dairyman's days start early.

Accustomed to setting my alarm for 4 o'clock each morning, it wasn't unusual to wake a few minutes before the buzzer in anticipation of a new day. Like my father, who followed in the footsteps of his father, I worked a small Mississippi dairy farm and drove a semitruck to make ends meet.

My routine each day began by tossing back the sheet and rolling out of bed. And it was a routine learned and practiced each working day for four decades: I shuffled across the floor toward the bathroom; took a long, hot shower to limber up joints that were stiff from many years of hard, physical labor; pulled on a pair of Wrangler jeans; and slipped on a long-sleeved tan cotton Henley. Then I'd put on a Timex and shove my feet into a pair of Justin leather work boots. The routine was so ingrained, I could have done it in my sleep and without ever stopping to think about it. But beginning April 9, 2004, nothing would ever be the same. And, I'll never take for granted the comforts found in the simple "routine" of life.

My "hooch" was a 12-foot-square room, part of a pre-fabricated metal building. From the outside, home appeared like the millions of tool sheds that sit in countless American backyards. Instead of housing lawn mowers and garden hoses, my home away from home at Camp Anaconda was a duplex structure among hundreds of others, each with two bedrooms that sandwiched a shared shower room in between.

On Iraq's liberation birthday I decided against breakfast and flipped on the television to catch the latest local news. The increase of militant attacks on both military units and civilian contractors gave the commentators on the Armed Forces Network plenty of news to report. Fallujah was in chaos, and there was always sporadic fighting around Baghdad. I wondered if our convoy would be allowed to make our run or if our routes would be altered because of the hostilities.

The television blared while I refreshed my bug-out bag, which is the backpack that contained a few essential items in case of an emergency and I had to "bug out" quickly.

Among other things, the bag contained a change of clothes, bottled water, and my only means of protection, an AK-47 bayonet purchased from an Iraqi outside the camp gate.

Next, I disposed of two empty water bottles from the day before and pulled out a few classic country music cassette tapes of George Jones and Merle Haggard. Even though the military trucks we were scheduled to drive that day were not equipped with tape players, I pitched the tapes back in the bag. A pair of Wrangler jeans, a brown cotton T-shirt, and a pair of white cotton crew socks went in next. The bayonet was the only weapon I was allowed to carry. I took it out of the bug-out bag every night and placed it on the table next to my bed for quick use in case militants broke into the camp. We were right next to the "wire," which is the fence that surrounded the camp, but gossip around the quarters told of break-ins and convinced me to find some means of protection. The bayonet went in last on top of the clothes for instant access.

Since all KBR employees are required to wear protective gear when they're outside the camp, the next thing I reached for was a flak vest. When not in use, it remained next to my military-style Kevlar helmet atop a crude clothes cabinet. Slipping the vest over my head, I fastened the Velcro straps on its sides, clipped a radio to the shoulder strap, and grabbed my helmet.

As a convoy commander, I had to report to the KBR security briefing at 6 o'clock each morning. We were briefed on the conditions outside the wire. The KBR security advisor told us he would have to go to the military side and check to see if the routes were still closed. The roads on our maps are color coded for the degree of danger. Roads coded red are off-limits, while roads designated amber are okay to travel. That morning, the security advisor informed us that all roads were red but said he would let us know when it changed. The day started like most others, with nothing unusual to report.

It crossed my mind that April 9, 2004, was the first anniversary of the day Baghdad fell to Coalition troops, marking the end of the Saddam Hussein regime. I remember watching the news as a crowd of Iraqis toppled the statue of Saddam. The jubilation of the Iraqi people that day told me we were doing the right thing.

Meanwhile, I went to the Total Safety Task Instruction (TSTI) meeting, along with other convoy commanders, our foremen, and drivers, to cover the roster of who was going out that day. I gathered all the men in my convoy and held a follow-up TSTI meeting with them. I explained the route we were taking and went over the road conditions. Just as our meeting wrapped up the KBR security advisor walked up to tell us the roads had been okayed and the designation changed to amber. I sensed that he was still worried about the way things seemed to be heating up, but there was always concern anytime we left the camp.

I felt like we declared victory a bit too soon in this conflict, but we had a duty to deliver fuel to our troops. We were all focused on the job at hand. There was no time to worry about what might happen or about things beyond our control.

The war was still going on and the fighting had gotten

more intense the past few weeks. One of our convoys was hit as it left one of the bases a few days earlier. The militants set off a series of improvised explosive devices, which the military called IEDs, and fired shots from small arms as the trucks drove by. They were extremely lucky that no one was killed or injured because six or seven rocket-propelled grenades, or RPGs, barely missed several trucks. Only one truck was hit with a single small-arms round. The kill zone — the stretch of road where militants fired their weapons at our convoys — was only about 100 yards long. Suppressing fire by the military escorts and the fact that they got out of range so quickly is probably what saved them.

Two convoys were scheduled to haul fuel that day, and we were assigned to drive camouflaged green military trucks. Mine was to be the first to push out. We had 17 systems, which are complete rigs comprised of a tractor and tanker trailer. The two tractor-only "bobtails" that accompanied us in the event of a breakdown rounded out our equipment needs for KBR's 20-man crew. Winding up the meeting, I reminded everyone to stay alert to the 100-meter spacing required between each truck. If the trucks were spaced too tightly the whole convoy could be lost to a chain of tanker explosions if only one IED or any other roadside bomb destroyed one of the trucks. If the trucks strayed too far apart, the security and organization of traveling in a convoy fell apart as well.

With the meeting concluded, everybody climbed in their

trucks and motored up to the staging line. Our trucks ready, we waited for the Army Reserve 724th Transportation Company security unit to join us. Their gun-trucks were big armor-plated, medium-duty, 5-ton tandem-axle units. The gun-trucks came equipped with either a Mark-19 grenade launcher or a .50-caliber machine gun mounted in their bed. Each of the gun-trucks transported three soldiers, two riding up front with guns pointing out the windows and one man manning the heavy weapon in the back.

Then the news came that our destination had changed. We were going to Baghdad International Airport (BIAP) instead of Webster. That was certainly no cause for alarm; it just meant there would be a delay while my foreman reworked the mission sheet. He hightailed it back to Transportation Operations and submitted the new report. When it was time to go, we were still waiting for the rest of our security detail to arrive. Since our protection unit was running behind, the supervisors decided to push out the second convoy first. Dust billowed as the trucks rolled through the gate and left the security of the camp.

Listening to the company radio I heard that the first convoy was turning around and coming back to camp. I didn't know why they were returning, but I soon found out they had not carried the required number of communications radios. Each convoy escort was required to have at least one in the front and one in the back.

About the time the first convoy got back, the rest of our security unit arrived and held yet another security briefing. They explained we would head southwest out of

Balad to main supply route (MSR) Tampa then proceed south through Taji to MSR Sword, turn west, go about two miles and turn south, which would take us straight into BIAP. I had not been to BIAP from Camp Anaconda, only from a different route that was located on the southwestern side of the base. Lieutenant Brown, the leader of military security for our convoy, said he had six men to ride on our trucks as shooters, so I put one in every other truck to ride shotgun. Positioning gun-trucks behind every third truck completed our security task. The lieutenant's Humvee was in the lead with another Humvee protecting the rear.

After all the waiting and changing of plans, we finally pulled out of the gates of Camp Anaconda in Balad around 10 in the morning to begin our 60-mile trek. The traffic was a little heavier than normal, and people were walking along the roadway. Our trucks were 100 meters apart, stretching the convoy out more than one mile.

Checking my rearview mirror, I watched as some of the drivers failed to maintain their 100-meter spacing. Two of our new drivers were having problems keeping the proper distance, which was a matter of survival. I didn't have enough drivers that morning; so three men had been dispatched from another department to join our crew. The new drivers had not been out before and were not used to running 100 meters apart. One of them kept falling too far behind. I keyed my radio every few minutes, coaching him into position. By the time we hit the freeway our spacing was correct.

Traveling westbound, just north of Baghdad, the free-way beneath us was similar to any six-lane interstate in the United States. We skirted the north side of Baghdad, never getting into the city. Shacks and rundown buildings dominated the areas along the freeway. Oddly, one of Saddam's palaces sat in the midst of a produce field sur-rounded by slums west of MSR Tampa. Staying alert for trouble, I recalled from our meeting that just south of Taji other convoys reported earlier attacks. Several overpasses and a pedestrian walkway crossing over the highway cre-ated ideal platforms for throwing rocks and shooting at trucks. With good reason, we had nicknamed that stretch of road "Widow Maker."

Beyond Widow Maker we called the next stretch of highway "Sniper Alley," because for the past six months, our convoys had been attracting small-arms fire from the slum houses along there. Farther along the route, where we merged onto MSR Sword, the military and KBR employees had named the road "IED Boulevard," which earned its notorious handle from local entrepreneurs, who often stand along the road selling black-market gasoline from one- and five-gallon cans.

An Iraqi motorist's version of full-service was to pull to the shoulder of the road and purchase a can of fuel. The seller just poured the gas in right there while the cus-tomer's car parked on the freeway. These gas salesmen often left their empty cans sitting along the road, but they weren't always empty. Often, when loaded with explo-sives and detonated from a remote location, these cans could easily be transformed into IEDs. Insurgents would link seven or eight cans together about 15 to 20 feet apart to create a daisy chain effect. If our trucks ran too close together, a daisy chain IED could destroy five or six trucks. On the other hand, if a cluster of gas-can IEDs were detonated and each truck was 100 meters apart, only one truck might be destroyed.

Gas cans were just one of the means for creating IEDs. Mortar rounds, artillery and tank projectiles, and in some cases, light rocket warheads were also used to construct daisy chains.

Our convoy drivers felt nothing more than normal apprehension, but that stretch of road soon proved that its reputation was well deserved.

Tommy gave a ration pack to this boy and his father.
Iraqi children often beg for handouts by the roadside.

Tommy and his fellow drivers wait for a final briefing at Camp Anaconda near the town of Balad.

CHAPTER 2

FRIDAY, APRIL 9, 2004
10:30 A.M.
IRAQ

"WE'RE TAKING FIRE"

The sight of abandoned gas cans sitting near the road wasn't anything new, so we continued rolling, ironically enough, down IED Boulevard. I had seen empty cans along the highway the entire six months I'd been in Iraq. We couldn't just turn around because a few gas cans sat on the side of the road. Still concerned about their ominous presence, I became more alert. Traffic was sparse, much less than I had seen on that road on earlier trips.

By 10:30, or so, the entire convoy was on the freeway. Right away the traffic started disappearing and when cars began swerving off the highway to get out of the way, I realized something was about to happen. We were trapped. There was no way we could turn around; the guardrail in the median prevented a U-turn.

Tommy Zimmerman, driving one of the trucks behind me, radioed, "I'm having trouble. The truck is dying on me, it's quitting." Although Tommy didn't say anything on the radio about taking fire, he was under attack. We had trucks break down all the time, trucks just quit. That's why we had two bobtails — trucks without a trailer — in the rear. The first gun-truck that got to a disabled truck pulled security by stationing a soldier on either side to watch for danger while another stood at the ready manning the big gun in the truck. A bobtail would then pull up to take the whole truck in tow or hook to the trailer as quickly as possible.

I radioed 1st Lt. Matt Brown of Bartonville, Illinois, the Army convoy commander, "I've got a truck that is breaking down. We need to get some gun support there with him."

"We're taking fire in the rear!" radioed one of our bobtails, either Stephen Fisher or Jackie Lester.

"We need to get this man picked up," I radioed back to the lieutenant. "Get the gun-truck to pick him up. Let's leave the truck, just get the men."

All at once everybody was on their radio reporting they were all taking fire. Instantly, our truck was slammed with the first rounds. But as the barrage of bullets continued, Nelson knew that speed would be the only thing to save us, and he smashed the accelerator to the floor.

We were under an assault like none other I had experienced. I'm no stranger to gunfire. Growing up in the country, it was normal to target practice out behind the barn, or in the backyard, for that matter, but the world is much different when the bullets are coming at you. It sounded like the truck was getting pounded with a hail of golf balls.

Never had the kill zone been so lengthy. Usually an ambush spanned only 100 yards or so in length, this one was endless. We had taken some small-arms fire before, maybe an RPG or an IED every now and then, but this was different. This was a massive, well-planned assault.

We were all pedal-to-the-metal, mash-it-to-the-floor. That's all we could do.

Lt. Brown radioed, "There's a truck on fire up ahead, we've gotta get off this road."

We veered off the freeway, through a hole our military had created in the guardrail, and onto the frontage road. Most of our trucks followed, but another convoy would follow us in 30 to 40 minutes. I needed to alert them before they traveled too far. I grabbed my Qualcomm on-board satellite computer from between the seats and held it in my lap. I had just started typing "convoy under attack" when a bullet slammed through the passenger-side door and struck my right forearm, knocking the computer out of my hands. There was no pain, though, only a strong jolt. A huge chunk of my arm had been blown away. Blood gushed from my arm and ran all over the computer.

I needed to find a way to stop the bleeding. I grabbed a pair of clean socks that had fallen out of my bug-out bag. I wrapped a sock around my arm and handed the radio to Nelson. "You are going to have to run communications until I can get the bleeding stopped," I shouted. The sock wasn't long enough to tie off so I just kept twisting it, hoping the pressure would slow the bleeding.

The gunfire was so loud. We were right next to the buildings from where the shooters were firing their weapons. Nelson screamed into the radio, but I couldn't understand a word he was saying over the noise from the mortar rounds and rocket-propelled grenades. We were being riddled with bullets, but we kept going.

For a truck having trouble, the standard operating procedure called for the driver to go as far as he could until the gun-truck could pick him up. Each truck driver was taught to stay calm and drive through the kill zone, get to a safe place, and assess personnel and equipment damage. At the very least our drivers were trained never to stop. The gun-trucks were there to take care of the disabled crews and pick them up. Everyone who was able had to keep running.

Our truck began breaking down, and other trucks were passing us. I could not see who was in the trucks and did not know which trucks had been disabled behind us. The trucks were completely out of order.

We crept along the frontage road maybe a mile from the exit that leads to BIAP. I noticed in the mirror that some of our trucks near the rear were still on the freeway and moving past us. Some trucks had passed us on the frontage road as well. They were doing what they were supposed to do. It was each driver's call; if the smoke cleared to where you could see, you drove through it as fast as you could. The trucks on the freeway were farther away from the small-arms fire, but since we were on the frontage road we were at point-blank range.

I could not see the shooters. They were hidden in the grass and behind buildings. Some fired from behind parked cars protected by a screen of women and children. Mortar rounds exploded in front of us; a black cloud of smoke followed each blast. A rocket-propelled grenade slammed into our truck. Our vehicle shook violently and nearly turned over.

Nelson yelled, "We've been hit by something — something big!"

I shouted back, "We gotta keep going!"

We were still moving forward, bullets hammering the truck. I just knew that at any moment our rig was going to explode and at any second we were going to die. We continued on, trucks still on the freeway were passing us; bullet holes riddled the huge tanks, literally unloading the fuel on the road. The trucks looked like water-sprinkler systems wetting down the pavement, which was slick with the oily diesel fuel. The trucks slid through like hogs on ice.

Other trucks continued speeding past, going as fast as their governed engines would allow. One of the drivers, however, lost control on the slippery road about a half-mile ahead of us. He fishtailed a little bit, flipped upside down, and his truck and trailer slid down into the median. An instant later the rig exploded. The whole truck blew up right there in front of us. The unfortunate driver didn't have a chance; it was over in a flash.

We limped along slower and slower while trucks continued going by. We were almost to the exit when I saw another truck at the ramp on its right side just off the frontage road in a ditch. I assumed the driver got off the ramp too fast, lost it, and rolled over. The whole top of the cab was mashed down.

We were barely moving, just crawling, maybe five to ten miles per hour. As we approached the truck I did not see any movement at all. Of course, we wanted to stop and help, but we had to continue. The gun-trucks would come along to care for them. Had we stopped, we would have blocked the entire road and stopped everybody behind us, who would then be sitting ducks for the gunmen.

When we reached the ramp, we began fishtailing and spinning out of control. "Nelson, we can't block this ramp," I shouted. "Try to get over to the guardrail as far as you can. If we spin out by the guardrail maybe another truck can still get by."

We managed to make it to the top of the ramp. Another truck swerved off the freeway onto our ramp, cut in front of us, and made a left-hand turn onto the crossover bridge. Another truck that had made the same turn looked to have been hit by a rocket, rolled over, and came to rest against the guardrail of the bridge. We slowly started across the bridge, over the freeway passing the disabled truck; there was no sign of life.

The truck that had just passed us was maybe 100 yards in front of us, moving fast, and getting farther away when it exploded, erupting into flames. Perhaps it ran into an anti-tank mine (who knows what happened), but the whole truck just blew up. Flames shot more than 200 feet into the air.

By then we were hardly moving at all, and the gunfire had not stopped. Out of nowhere Army Specialist Gregory Goodrich ran and jumped up next to me on the running board of our truck, wrapped his left arm around the mirror and yelled, "We have got to drop this trailer."

"We are losing air pressure, must've happened when that big explosion hit us, must've knocked out our brakes," Nelson yelled.

We were dragging our trailer like an anchor, but the slick roads allowed the trailer to skid along. As much gunfire as we were taking, there was no way Nelson or I could get out of the truck. Whoever got out would have been shot to death. We pushed ahead. I looked over Specialist Goodrich's shoulder toward the buildings; all I could see were AK-47s sticking out around the corners. I didn't see a soul, just all those guns stuck out and firing. I felt at any minute the brave soldier would be cut down.

He was just standing up on the running board and had absolutely no protection. He was shot in the arm but kept firing away and trying to hold on. A couple of times he grabbed another clip, bumped it, and slammed it in his M-16. He was sweeping his gun back and forth and firing, not really picking his targets. He realized he needed a better rest, a better support for his rifle. He swung around and climbed onto the hood of the truck to fire from a prone position. Using it as a rest, he continued firing at anything that moved. We steadily crept along, barely moving at all. We were coming up on one of the trucks that had exploded, and it was still blazing.

"We can't go by that truck," Nelson yelled. We'll catch fire, too."

He was right; fuel was spewing from both sides of our tank. We couldn't stop there, though. And, we were right in the middle of a gunfight.

"This truck's fixin' to die," Nelson yelled again. "It's fixin' to quit!"

We had no more choices. We had to bale. Right then a Humvee pulled around in front of us at about 100 feet and stopped. Then Specialist Goodrich rolled off the hood of our truck and fell to the ground, picked himself up, and ran for the Humvee. Nelson was running right behind him. Nelson dove through the right door right behind the soldier. I ran as hard as I could toward the back of the Humvee and was within 10 steps when the driver gunned the engine and sped away. Loaded down with a heavy flak vest, a 4-pound helmet, and wounded, there was no way I was going to catch up. I hollered but knew they'd never hear me. They never checked up. They just drove away.

There was no question that I was in a bad situation standing there in the road. Bullets were still flying from all directions. I flashed back to what my Vietnam-veteran roommate in Kuwait told me, "If you are ever under fire, you get down on the ground as quick as you can and stay down." I did exactly that, maintaining a low profile and searching for an escape route. The buildings were close and I thought that maybe I was near the outer edge of the kill zone. I thought, *Maybe I can make it to one of those hous-*

es without getting shot. But then I saw a bunch of people running toward me. I got down low and tried pulling myself in the direction of one of the houses, but my right arm was useless. I could not pull myself forward with it at all.

So, I tried rolling, but it was not easy, either. I managed to roll about halfway to the buildings when I noticed a couple of teenage boys between two of the structures. They were pointing across the road, hollering and screaming something in Arabic. I had stopped rolling and watched the boys to see what they were doing. I could still hear gunfire.

Looking back at the road to see what held the boys' attention, I could see an Iraqi man wearing a dark tan robe, crouched down, and aiming an AK-47 right at me. He poked his weapon at me like he wanted me to do something. I didn't understand. He made the pushing motion again, over and over. Both of my hands were above my head, as I got ready to roll again. I held them higher to show him I did not have a weapon. Then I realized I still held my satellite phone in my left hand. He thought it was a gun, so I dropped it to the ground.

He approached me slowly as the two boys raced toward me. They got to me before the gunman and immediately began stripping me of my helmet, flak vest, and wristwatch. They took my wallet from the right hip pocket of my jeans, my ID badge from the left, and change from the front-right pocket.

I did not know if the man was going to shoot me or not. Six to eight more people were coming from across the road. They gathered around, pulled me up, and began walking me up a short slope. As soon as we reached the top I saw a crowd of 20 or more people coming toward me from an alley. They charged straight at me. One of the young men in the crowd was holding a rifle high above his head with the butt end pointing down. I knew what that meant; I was about to get it across the head. I turned my face away, but he struck me diagonally across my right temple and ear. The blow hurt, but did not knock me out. The crowd was frantic, shouting, and yelling in Arabic.

I did not know what their plans were for me, but I was well aware of the mutilation of the four security officers in Fallujah. They were acting like I was a big prize or trophy. They were either going to show me off or kill me like they did the guys in Fallujah. *Were they going to burn my body, hang me, and video it for television?* All of these questions flashed through my mind. But I was not afraid. It would have done no good at that point to get hysterical. There was nothing I could do; I had no control of the situation.

In next to no time, a small, light gray car raced up, and four guys jumped out and started screaming in Arabic at the crowd. They pulled me around and shoved me into the backseat of the car. Two of them got in the front seat and one on either side of me. They backed out and headed in the same direction the convoy was going, but they went one block over, made a left turn, and drove east on a dirt road in the opposite direction the convoy was headed.

The passenger in the front seat held his weapon out the window and hollered, "*Amreeky! Amreeky! Amreeky!*" I assumed he meant, "We have an American." People were walking on both sides of the road just looking at us as he kept hollering, "*Amreeky! Amreeky! Amreeky!*" We soon turned left and crossed the freeway very close to the rear of my convoy. Some of our trucks were turned over and on fire. Plumes of oil soot floated across the sky as far as I could see.

The brutality of the attack hit me; I knew a lot of men in my convoy died. Some of the men had been in Iraq only a month, two months at the most. Jackie Lester was the only man in the convoy who had been there longer than me. I was so saddened by the carnage and livid at the same time. I didn't know it yet, but five of my drivers were killed, and two are still missing. Steven Hulett of Manistee, Michigan; Jeffery Parker of Lake Charles, Louisiana; Jack Montague of Pittsburg, Illinois; Tony Johnson from Riverside, California and Stephen Fisher of York, Nebraska were killed. Timothy Bell from Mobile, Alabama, and William Bradley of Galveston, Texas, are still unaccounted for.

The 724th Army Transportation Company sustained heavy losses as well. Months later I learned that Specialist Gregory Goodrich, the soldier who defended my truck, was shot and killed a few minutes after he dove into the Humvee that rescued my driver. Sergeant Elmer C. Krause of Greensboro, North Carolina, died during the attack. Private First Class Keith "Matt" Maupin of Batavia, Ohio, is still listed as missing in action and feared dead.

My captors turned onto the same frontage road I had

ridden on a few minutes before. The driver pushed the lit-tle car to its limits. We must have been going around 80 miles per hour; he was driving frantically. I was afraid he was going to wreck the car.

I lowered my head to look through the windshield and saw an Apache helicopter hovering high above us. I fig-ured the Apache would see that little car driving errati-cally past the burning trucks, think it had something to do with the attack, and decide to take us out. I leaned for-ward, pointed upward between the driver and passenger, and said, "That helicopter is going to shoot us. You come down through here this fast and they are going to shoot us." The driver must have understood because he quickly wheeled into the carport of a small house. We rushed inside, startling the occupants.

They sat me down, removed my boots and bloody shirt, and, for the first time, examined my injury. One of the men brought in a strip of cotton cloth and wrapped my arm. I grabbed my boots and struggled to put them back on. I tried to get one of my feet down into the boot without using my hands, but I kept losing my balance and stumbling around. The front-seat passenger, whom I would come to know later as Tiger, slipped his sandals off and told me to put them on. He took my boots and claimed them for his own. Another one of my captors threw me a long-sleeved black shirt. Gently easing a sleeve over my right arm, I slowly worked the shirt over and around the rest of my upper body.

I was ordered back to the car where they covered my

head with a hood or head wrap in an attempt to blindfold me. The cloth almost covered my eyes, but I could still see. We took off again, heading west on the frontage road past all the burning trucks. In the distance I saw several men standing around a Chevrolet Suburban parked in the road. As we got closer I could see that one of the men was wearing a blue flak vest, just like mine. I hoped they might be able to help me. As we approached I noticed the words "TV Crew" in white letters on the back of the jacket. I knew then they would be of no help. I became very angry; the closer we got the madder I became. The fact that they were filming all of that destruction really enraged me.

We pulled around them and stopped. The TV crew hurried over. The man sitting to my left got out of the car, leaving the door open. Because one of the men in the crew looked Arabic, I assumed the TV crew was with a network such as al-Arabia or al-Jazeera. I refused to look at them. I was irate that they were there. They may have been there in good faith, but I didn't think they needed to be filming the devastation of my convoy. I wondered if the crew knew in advance the attack was going to happen. It was very suspicious that they just happened along.

I learned later that they were reporters for the Australian Broadcasting Company who had spotted the cloud of smoke from our burning tank trucks and had raced to the scene of the ambush. My captors had spotted them and stopped to show off their prize.

Out of the corner of my eye I could see the camera stuck in the door opening, with the reporter standing behind the cameraman. The masked gunman to my right snatched the white hood off my head and shoved my cheek to force me to look at the camera.

"What happened?" the reporter asked.

"They attacked our convoy," I growled. "That's all I'm going to say." I turned and lowered my head. I was consumed with a white-hot rage for the news crew. I felt they were taking advantage of the situation. They were capitalizing on my misery and that of everyone in my convoy. I did not want to talk to them at all.

"Do you want to give us your name?" the reporter asked.

"Huh?" as I turned to face them again.

"Do you want to give us your name?" the reporter repeated.

"Hamill. Thomas."

I looked forward as a gunman jumped in beside me and slammed the door as they sped off.

I realized then that there was nothing I could physically do. I couldn't control my destiny. I said a silent prayer:

God, you are going to have to intervene in this situation. There's nothing I am going to be able to do. I have no control. You're going to have to take care of everything from this point on until I am rescued or released. I have to lay all of this at your feet, at the cross, because there is nothing I can do to change my outcome with these people.

Though I was angry, I was not afraid. I was not about to show fear to those people. They thrive on fear.

As we turned north and headed away from BIAP, I looked over my right shoulder at the charred mass of wreckage that defined my convoy. The road eventually wound through a rural area, and people were walking on both sides of the highway. All of them were carrying weapons, and it was the middle of the day. Some of them had satchels on their backs with four or five RPGs sticking out. *What's going on?* I wondered. *Why are we not blowing the dickens out of this place? I am sure somebody's seeing all these people out here. And here we are driving right into the middle of them.*

We passed a sandbagged bunker lined with armed men hunkered down in a grassy ditch. They must have been some of the ones firing on our convoy. The driver sped recklessly at 75 to 80 miles per hour. The car rocked back and forth as he rounded curves without slowing down. I was sure we were all going to die in a car wreck.

We came to a small village with some stores and small buildings along the road. We made a right turn and followed a six-foot-tall block wall on our left for several hundred feet. As the wall ended we came upon a big open area, and three or four cars were leaving. We veered away from them as if my captors didn't want them to see me.

Houses surrounded the square. As we pulled into a driveway, about a dozen Iraqi men were standing outside. They stared at me as we walked inside. We passed through the foyer, turned left through another door, and walked through two large rooms. We settled in a room in the far corner of the building. They laid me down on a pad stretched across the floor. About 20 Iraqi men stood around me, staring, talking to each other, and muttering words in Arabic that I did not understand.

The captors led another man into the room, and he carried a large yellow plastic bag that appeared to be full of medical supplies. He walked over to me and pulled out an IV line and drip bag. I guessed he was a field doctor of sorts. He unwrapped the makeshift bandage from my arm, and for the first time I saw just how bad the injury was. A large sheet of skin and muscle, about the size of my hand, had been sheered off and just hung down, attached only by a two-inch strip of skin. It was a bloody mess. The field doctor positioned it back, rewrapped it, and started the IV in my left arm, on the inside of the elbow.

The crowd of men scrutinized me the entire time the doctor worked. I did not say a word; I just looked back at them blank-faced. Standing across the room was a tall, thin, one-armed man about six feet, four inches tall. My eyes were locked on him as he wove his way through the crowd and stopped in front of me. I saw that his right arm was missing above his elbow. He stood over me for a while looking at me; I just looked back. He swiftly raised his left arm, clinched his fist, and shouted, "By the hand of Mohammad, I will hang you from the bridge in Fallujah tomorrow! By *my* hand I will hang you from the bridge in Fallujah tomorrow!"

I just looked him straight in the eye and said nothing. He turned and walked away.

The crowd of men left later that afternoon. Directly,

my four escorts lifted me up and ushered me out to the car. We hit the road again. I held my drip bag as we drove a short distance to a small building that was about 10 feet wide and 20 feet long. The first thing I noticed as we entered the room was an iron bed with a rope hanging from the ceiling near its edge. They laid me down on the bed, took my drip bag and tied it to the rope.

FEEEWWW... FEEEWWW... Two rockets, aimed toward BIAP, blasted off with a roar from just outside the building where I was being held. Earlier, our convoy had taken rounds from this place. I couldn't believe they were firing rockets from the yard of that building, and there I was laying in one of their launch sites. Our forces could have easily destroyed that building.

I could only lie there; there was no other choice. I knew that the images of me sitting in the back of that car would be shown on every network television station in America. My kids were going to see it and be afraid for me. I could just see them sitting there watching and not knowing what the future held. I thought about my wife, her health, and how she was going to handle the news.

Then there was the uncertainty of what had happened to the men in my convoy. I was sure that there had been loss of life. *Who?* I wondered, *How is the media going to frame this?* Would the coverage make this seem even worse to my family? I wanted to think of my family, but I could not permit my thoughts to be only of them. If I worried about them constantly I might panic and do something foolish that would cause my captors to kill me. I asked

God to take away the worry, and he did.

The loss of blood sapped my strength. I became very sleepy and eventually I dozed off for maybe three or four hours. When I awoke it was dark. I lay there until the men came in to get me for another car ride.

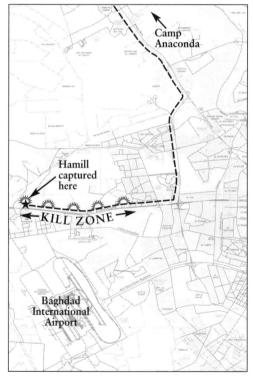

Thomas Hamill's convoy (dashed line) was ambushed along a nearly eight-mile stretch of the Abu Ghrab Expressway.

Specialist Gregory F. Goodrich of the
724th Transportation Company,
U.S. Army Reserve.

Iraqis charge across the road past the burning
wreckage of a fuel tanker, one of the trucks
in Tommy's convoy ambushed on April 9.

CHAPTER 3

FRIDAY,
APRIL 9, 2004
MACON, MISSISSIPPI

THE PHONE CALL

Kellie Hamill stirred slightly, suspended in the dreamy fog between asleep and awake. "I began to sense Tommy's presence and warmth beside me,"Kellie said. "The feeling grew stronger by the second, my curiosity built up, my heart rate increased. 'Why is he here now?' I wondered. 'What is he doing home?' I turned over and Tommy was lying beside me, I could not believe he was here. 'What are you doing home, in bed?' I asked."

"I just wanted to let you know that I am okay. I am alive," he said.

Kellie reached out to touch him and was jolted awake. Opening her eyes, she looked over to see her 12-year-old daughter, Tori, still asleep. The dream was so real that Kellie lay there for a few moments to regain her senses. She stared at Tori just to make sure it was her daughter and not Tommy.

Kellie got up and walked across the room as the phone began to ring. Tommy's mother, Phyllis Hamill, who lives with Tommy's family, answered the call in the next room. It was Tommy's 93-year-old grandmother, Vera Hamill, whom everyone affectionately called Maw Maw, and she was asking some frantic questions. Phyllis called Kellie to the living room and began relaying the questions. "Maw Maw saw on the news that an American convoy has been attacked. Where is Tommy today? Do you think it was his convoy?" Maw Maw was full of questions that Kellie couldn't answer.

"If Tommy's convoy was involved we would have been notified," Kellie assured them. "He assured me before he left we would get a phone call if anything ever happened, and nobody has called."

Kellie shuffled back through the house to wake Tori and her 13-year-old son, Thomas. The day's plan centered around running errands. Kellie promised to take Tori and Tori's friend Ashley Nelson to Columbus, because each girl needed to purchase a pair of cleats for softball. Thomas stayed behind with Ashley's brother, Tony.

Thomas and Tori climbed into the backseat of Kellie's 1995 red Ford Thunderbird, and Phyllis rode shotgun. After picking up Ashley and leaving Thomas, Kellie started the 30-minute drive to Columbus. It was a beautiful spring day with a temperature hovering around 75 degrees. Traffic was light on the highways leading from Macon to Columbus. Though Kellie wasn't overly concerned, she could not get the convoy attack out of her mind.

"Just as we took the exit to Columbus, shortly after

noon, my cell phone rang," Kellie recalled.

"Kellie, this is Phillip Campbell with KBR in Houston. Are you where you can talk?" the voice on the other line said.

"'No, not at the moment, but give me a minute and I will be.' I responded as my heart raced. I pulled across two lanes without looking for oncoming traffic, into a sign company's parking lot. All the spaces were occupied, so I just stopped in the middle of the vehicles.

"'Okay, I'm parked now,' I said as I threw the gear shift into park. 'What's the matter?'"

"Tommy's convoy has been attacked," he stated. "We aren't sure right now, but it looks like at least seven men are missing."

"What about Tommy? What about Tommy?" Kellie cried.

"We aren't sure yet, but right now he is unaccounted for."

"What happened, what's going on?" Tommy's mother began shouting.

Kellie sobbed uncontrollably as Mr. Campbell continued explaining the situation, "It will be at least 24 hours before we will know exactly who is missing. During an attack everybody scatters. They get into other trucks, Humvees, and gun-trucks. They will wind up at other camps. In 24 hours we should be able to make a roll call, and I'll call you back just as soon as we know something further."

"Thank you, call me as soon as you can," Kellie begged.

Kellie sobbed. She could not tell Phyllis for a minute or so. Kellie calmed down and began recounting what Mr. Campbell had said when she realized Tori was sitting in the backseat. "I had totally forgotten she was back there," Kellie said. "She was bawling her heart out. 'Is Daddy okay?'"

"I don't know, Tori," Kellie answered through the tears.

Kellie pulled out of the parking lot, turned north on Highway 45, whipped into a Shell station, and said she had to go to the restroom. "I grabbed my cell phone and hurried inside," Kellie said. "When I got inside the restroom I called my father. My first instinct and thought was, 'I need my daddy.' My daddy could reach out to the Lord better than I could, and prayer was what was needed then." Kellie failed to reach her father by phone.

"All I wanted to do was go home," Kellie recalled. "I got back in the car and headed back toward Macon." While speeding down the road, Kellie called Ashley's dad, Mike Nelson, and asked him to meet them at the intersection of Highways 45 and 14 with Thomas and to pick up Ashley. "I just told him that there was a problem," Kellie said. "I didn't want to talk about it while driving and get me and everybody in the car upset again. He didn't ask any questions and said he'd be there."

Normally a 30-minute drive, Kellie made it in much less time. "Why the Highway Patrol didn't stop us I will never know," Kellie said. "I met Mike and briefly explained what I knew. When Thomas got in the car I could tell he knew something was wrong. Tori cried and Thomas went silent. I told him about his dad and that we really didn't know anything yet. I tried to assure him that his dad would be all right. I wasn't so sure. Thomas did not say a word, he just stared straight ahead."

Kellie called several friends during her drive home. She called Tommy's best friend Jesse Green and volunteer fire chief Jerry Britt to tell them Tommy was missing.

Jerry was waiting at the house when Kellie and the children pulled up. She raced inside and found "1" blinking on the answering machine. Kellie frantically jabbed at the playback button hoping for a message from Tommy or from someone else saying he was okay. Kellie groaned when she recognized Aunt Coleene's voice asking for a return call.

Kellie called her father, Wallace Green, again and finally got through. "I broke down when I heard his voice and hysterically told him, 'Tommy's convoy has been attacked and he's missing. Help me, Daddy. Please help me. I don't know what to do. Can you pray for him?'"

"Everything's going to be okay," Kellie's father said calmly. "God has a hand in this. There is a reason Tommy's been captured. I have to get in touch with God. I have to go pray. I have to get the answers."

"We all just sat around the television flipping between the different news channels hoping to get new information about Tommy and his convoy," Kellie recalled. "Later, Jesse and Jerry went home. I went to bed about one in the morning and kept watching TV. Coleene stayed in the living room in front of that TV all night.

"I started thinking all sorts of crazy things. Tommy had told me before he left that there was a good chance he would never come home." Kellie's mind raced. *How am I going to live without him? How do I tell my children? This is not supposed to be happening; we are supposed to be together until we are old. Am I going to be alone forever and ever? Are the kids going to be without a father?*

Kellie kept driving herself to the brink of hysteria. *Was he lying somewhere in a lot of pain?*

"The unknown was killing me," Kellie said, "but then I thought back to my dream. The Lord must have known I needed to see Tommy at that exact time. He knew the dream would help me cope with the news of Tommy being reported missing. I thought back to a conversation I had with my father before Tommy left the first time for Iraq. Daddy said he would pray for the Lord to put a shield around him to keep him safe no matter what happened. I prayed the same way. I asked for a shield, or angels, or whatever it took to keep him from harm."

At approximately four in the morning Fox News Channel ran a short video clip that showed a man sitting in the back of a car with a masked gunman, but the man's face was blurred out. The news anchor said the man was taken hostage from a KBR convoy. "I got chills," Kellie said. "It flashed on and off so quickly I didn't have time to study the man."

Kellie surfed the news networks on DirecTV. CNN ran the clip a few minutes later. Then Fox News Channel showed it again. "Each time I studied the faceless man in the back of the car looking for anything that would tell me he was Tommy," Kellie said. "I got out of bed and just stood on the floor in front of the TV, staring at the screen, waiting for the next clip to be shown. It didn't stay on long enough to study it completely. It never crossed my mind to put a tape in the VCR and record it. Again Fox ran it, but I still could not tell. Then about 6:30 Fox showed it again, that time I focused on the man's hands. A rush came over my body. It was Tommy!

The clue was his left thumb, which was visible on the videotape. When Tommy was young he got his hands caught in a cement mixer and it chewed up his left thumb pretty badly. His thumbnail grows in a peculiar way over the end of the thumb. I could barely see it, but it sure looked like that man's thumb showed that oddity.

I recognized the way he held his arms, too. His right hand was tucked under his left bicep while his cupped left hand supported his right elbow. He held his thumb over the front part of his other elbow. Both arms were tight against his stomach. After being married to Tommy for 16 years, I recognize those little details about him. Since rotator cuff surgery in 2002 he always folded and held his arms the same way the man in the car was holding his. I was convinced the guy in the back of that car was Tommy and no one else."

Kellie studied every detail. She saw the blue jeans were faded, like Tommy's. Her experience as emergency medical responder told Kellie the stains on Tommy's jeans were not grease or oil, but blood! *That's an awful lot of blood,* she worried. "I just didn't want to think that one person could lose that much blood. Maybe he got it from trying to help someone else get out of a vehicle."

Kellie cried tears of joy. "He is alive," Kellie rejoiced. "The Lord was saying to me, 'I have your husband, he's alive, he's hurt, but he is okay.' The Lord had taken him out of a brutal assault and was not going to let him die over there. It was extremely difficult; I struggled with so many questions. I even questioned God for a few days." Kellie wondered, why did the Lord allow him to come home for her surgery in February to take him from me on April 9th?

The guilt that Kellie felt was almost overwhelming. "If only I'd been stronger and had been able to go through my surgery without bringing him home and let him do his job none of this would have happened to him. Had Tommy not come home for my surgery, he would have been home on his normal leave, beginning April 1st. He would not have been in that convoy."

Kellie thought back to when Tommy left to return to Iraq after her open-heart surgery. "I was not happy with his decision to go back," she said. "He had a job to do and I supported him, but letting him go was hard. Tommy would not have been happy if I had tried to make him stay. There was no way to stop him, and I would not have even tried if I could."

Still recovering from surgery a few weeks earlier, Kellie was unable to accompany Tommy on his 125-mile drive to the airport in Jackson, Mississippi; so she kissed him and waved good-bye as he and Jerry Britt drove away. "I cried for two hours after he left," she said. "I missed him terribly. I regretted not telling him how I really felt about him returning to Iraq."

Kellie remembered the last conversation she had with Tommy on April 7th, two days before the attack on his convoy. "I told him I had a bad feeling that something was going to go wrong," she said. "I cried to him to come home and kept telling him how worried I was for his safety. He asked, 'Do I sound worried?'

"No," I admitted. "And he told me, 'When I sound worried, then you need to worry.'"

"I pulled myself together, told him I loved him, and said good-bye, not realizing that would be the last time we would speak for quite some time."

Kellie was sitting in bed flipping between news channels when the phone rang at 8:30 in the morning. "It had been a little more than 20 hours since I last talked with Mr. Campbell," she recalled. "Before he could say anything I said, 'I know. It's him. I know he's the man in the back of that car.' He wanted to know how I knew, and I told him it was his hands and the way he was holding his arms. He didn't say anything for a while, and then he confirmed the man was indeed Tommy."

Dialing the phone, Kellie called her father to give him an update. "Not knowing what they may be doing to the man I love was very tough to deal with," Kellie said. "Tommy is my whole life, the father of my children, and I was scared the attackers were hurting him. I was too familiar with the beatings, mutilations, and burnings of the four workers in Fallujah. My world was crumbling."

*Thomas Hamill and his captors were filmed and
interviewed by Australian TV reporters
shortly after the attack.*

Phyllis Hamill, Tommy's mother,
was with Kellie when the call came
saying Tommy was missing.

Tommy with Kellie's parents, Georgia and Wallace Green.

CHAPTER 4

SATURDAY,
APRIL 10, 2004
IRAQ

"You Have Angered These People"

Sometime during the early morning we all loaded up in the same gray car and rode back to the building we had left a few hours earlier. We walked back through the foyer and turned left into a large room. A crowd of 18 to 20 Iraqi men were waiting and watching my every step. All the lights were on and the men were just standing around talking to each other. When I saw a video camera sitting atop a cardboard box, I knew they were going to make a tape.

One of the men motioned for me to sit on the floor. Another character I hadn't seen before, a clean-cut, well-dressed man, wearing shiny dark brown pants and a light tan shirt, sat down beside me. He was just over six feet tall, heavy-set, and spoke fairly good English. He said he had a list of questions and commanded me to answer them on camera. "Read these questions on this paper," he demanded. "I don't want you to read from the paper. When we turn the camera on, I want you to answer the questions that you have read."

I immediately thought they would ask questions I did not want to answer. I made my mind up that I was not going to answer any questions that would harm any of the KBR employees or the Department of Defense.

The questions were all about me; my name, age, where I was from, and what I was doing in Iraq. I was willing to answer those questions. One of the men picked up the camera and gave me the go-ahead.

"My name is Thomas Hamill. I am 43 years old. I am from Macon, Mississippi and I work for a contractor that supports the military. God bless."

"Why did you say that?" scoffed the man who had given me the questions.

"I am alive. God has blessed me today."

"You have angered these people," he said.

They all looked wide-eyed, and nobody said anything until the man with the questions told me to be still and not move. He went over to the cameraman who was anxiously trying to rewind the tape and erase "God bless." He finally got it rewound. They played it back, but it was still on the tape. He went through the process a second and third time. Each time they replayed the tape "God bless" was still there. They were visibly frustrated. I thought to myself, *God is not going to let them remove his name. It is there for good.* I was actually having a little fun with their predicament.

The other men were upset with the cameraman; I thought they were going to lynch him. Ten minutes passed before he finally managed to erase "God bless."

The room got quiet as one of the men, speaking in Arabic, began recording a statement. I knew he was making a demand of some sort. I later learned the translation of what he had said, which was, "Our only demand is to remove the siege from the City of Mosques. If you don't respond within 12 hours... he will be treated worse than those who were killed and burned in Fallujah." Maybe it was best I did not understand him.

The man, whose questions I answered, escorted me to the same car, and they shoved me into the backseat. We traveled a short distance to a small abandoned house and walked inside. Using a kerosene lantern to light the way, we entered to find the floors covered with filth, and I noticed two small windows covered with bars. The man brought in a thin pad and blanket and told me to sit down. He sat next to me and said, "You have angered these people with this 'God bless.' I don't know what they are going to do with you. They may kill you now."

I didn't say anything. I just sat there.

"I am going to leave a guard outside the door. He is a young man, but if you try to escape or make a noise, he will come in and kill you. In the morning if you need water or food call to him, and he will bring water and food."

He turned and shuffled out of the room, taking the lantern with him. Sitting on my pad in total darkness, I leaned against the wall and contemplated my plight. I never imagined that I would be kidnapped and held hostage. There was always a chance I could be killed. In fact, months before, I tried to prepare myself and my wife, Kellie, for that possibility. I was convinced that remaining calm in the face of my enemies was essential for my survival. I could not anger them nor show them fear. I had to adapt to whomever was guarding me, making demands, or giving orders. Each individual would have to be handled differently. I prayed:

God, I don't know what your plan is. I don't know if I am to die here or I am to live and go home to my family. Either way I know I am saved. I know if I die I will go to a better place. I know it is going to be bad for my family, but I am ready.

For some reason I felt I had been drawn to Iraq. Yes, I went for the money to save my farm, but I did not think I was being led there to die.

I thought back to a dream I had about 15 years earlier while away from home. I was driving a truck, working long hours, and not getting much rest. I parked my truck in a rest area one night to get some sleep. I dreamed I drove into a war-torn desert country, just like Iraq. Roads stretched for long distances through the hot open desert. I drove through the country, then turned around and came back out. I saw men firing guns and rockets, people running frantically in the streets, and smoke billowing all around. I had the feeling someone was after me, chasing me, but I was not involved in the fighting. The drive was crystal clear, but the fighting was off to the side, kind of foggy. I woke with a start in a cold sweat. That dream was so intense, so realistic, and so lifelike that I thought I had actually taken my truck and driven into that country. I climbed down from my truck to make sure it was just a dream.

After recalling that dream I thought it might be a sign that I would not die in Iraq. I prayed:

God, I don't know why you have chosen me, but I am going to pray for you to put a shield around me. I pray for you to send some angels to watch over me.

I knew God had control. I was going to take it one day at a time. I was not going to worry about a week down the road or even tomorrow.

Later that night and to the east, I heard the long, deep, drawn-out distant roar of an Abrams tank firing. Then I heard a steady, sustained, thud, followed by a rip of rapid fire from a Bradley fighting vehicle. They were searching in my direction, getting closer by the minute. The building began to shake. I pulled the blanket over my face as window glass shattered and fell to the ground. I wondered if the insurgents had brought me here knowing our military would come through and blow up my prison.

The building continued to shake, but the rounds were not close enough to harm me. Soon the bombardment stopped. Before long, I heard the tanks driving on the road in front of the house. Just after they passed, they started firing again. The shooting faded into the night, only to return and head back my way. The battle raged for hours as the soldiers beat the brush for Iraqi insurgents, searching them out like rabbits. Again, they closed the distance, passed, faded away, turned around, and came right back. I would later see that a canal ran past the house and through the desert. Sandbag emplacements along the canal had hidden the insurgents that the American soldiers had been hunting.

Once, I could hear only the Bradley firing single rounds. The tanks were approaching from the east, and I could tell they were getting closer when several AK-47s suddenly opened up on the Bradley. The insurgents had decided to attack with their assault weapons. The Bradley responded with a flurry of rapid fire for about 30 seconds and put an end to the AK-47 fire.

The tanks fired sporadically during the night, right up until sunrise. I listened to them off and on all night and didn't get much sleep. During the quiet moments, I knew that thinking about my family was not the smart thing to dwell upon. I knew that fretting about things that were beyond my control might cloud my thinking and cause me to take some drastic action that might get me killed.

Thomas Hamill sits in front of an Iraqi flag in a video image made by his captors who demanded that American forces withdraw from Fallujah.

An M-1A1 Abrams tank
moves into position somewhere in Iraq.

ULTIMATUM OF DEATH

Saturday mornings in the Hamill house were typical of most American families. They caught up on work around the house, ran errands, and took it easy. But April 10, 2004, was not a typical Saturday. Indeed, it would be the most difficult day the Hamill's had ever faced.

Kellie had not slept, haunted by Tommy's image on the television every 10 minutes. "I truly thought I was having a nightmare," she said. "All I wanted was to wake up and make it go away. My heart rate reached 132 beats per minute. The doctors told me it shouldn't get over 80 beats per minute. If the pressure in my heart was too great I could blow out the new valve and the repaired aneurysm. I had to take care of myself so I could be strong for Tommy, the kids, and my family."

Kellie's best friend, Doris Yoder, and Aunt Coleene came to the house about midmorning, and Jesse returned soon after. They were concerned about Kellie's health and her lack of sleep or food for the past 24 hours. "Doris is a nurse and immediately began monitoring my blood pressure and heart rate," Kellie said. "I don't know if I could have made it without those two wonderful ladies and Jesse. They insisted I eat and get some rest."

The adults reassured Kellie and the conversation soon turned to her feelings of guilt. "They kept telling me that I could not blame myself, that I had no control and did not cause the attack," Kellie said. "We were all concerned about the kids and decided we needed to keep them busy and allow them to carry on a normal life." Thomas coped with his pain by retreating to his room, while Tori clung to her mother seeking reassurance.

By midafternoon their emotional roller coaster raced downhill. The TV beckoned with a news alert, "The militants are now threatening to kill Thomas Hamill if their terms aren't met within twelve hours." Kellie tried to send Tori out of the room, but before she could leave the Iraqi militants quoted their ultimatum, "Our only demand is to remove the siege from the City of Mosques. If you don't respond within twelve hours... he will be treated worse than those who were killed and burned in Fallujah."

Tori came unglued emotionally again. "She did not need to hear something like that about her father," Kellie said regretfully. "Thomas was still in his room and didn't hear the news alert. He did not want to get anywhere near a television that was set to the news. It wasn't long before he found out on his own. He understood the magnitude of the situation. I'm not sure Tori really did, she just knew her daddy was in trouble."

Overwhelmed, Kellie stood in the middle of the room, numbed by the shocking news that her husband might be murdered in 12 hours.

Jerry Britt stopped by the Hamill residence later that afternoon. He and Jesse tried to calm down Kellie by reminding her of her training as a 911 dispatcher. "When I am on a call, I shut off all my emotions and show no feelings," Kellie said. "That is how I have been trained, and it is the only way to get through some of the tougher calls, especially those involving children." But Jerry's and Jesse's attempts did little to pacify Kellie's emotions.

Realizing that a media frenzy was coming, the close-knit community went to work to hold reporters at bay. Sheriff's deputies cordoned off the Hamill house with yellow crime-scene tape. Others removed the road sign that identified the Hamill residence. "I wanted to buy as much time as I could for me and my children," Kellie said. "I did not want to talk to the media. And I sure did not want Thomas and Tori to have to show their emotions in public or deal with news reporters, either."

Expecting a wave of media, and with the uncertainty of what might appear on the news next, Doris, Coleene, Jesse, and Kellie discussed their options. They decided it would be safest to take the kids out of school and send them to Doris's for a while. "I didn't want the media to be able to recognize them," Kellie reasoned. "I wanted the kids out of the house before the media started showing up. I got the kids ready, and Doris took them to her house."

Scott Boyd, publisher of the *Macon Beacon*, called late that afternoon to warn Kellie that the media was about to descend upon their house. He informed Kellie that some of the national media was in Jackson and starting their hunt. Scott offered to come to the Hamill home, not for a story, but to help in any way he could. "Scott cut himself off from being a reporter and became a valued friend," Kellie recalled. "He stayed with us for quite a while detailing what the media would want and how they would go about getting information."

The small measures the Hamills and their friends had taken to place a buffer between themselves and the media had little effect. Journalists from all facets of the media quickly learned the location of the Hamill home. They seemed to swarm around the house before descending on their quarry Saturday night.

CHAPTER
6

**SUNDAY,
APRIL 11, 2004
IRAQ**

PARCHED
COUNSELOR

On the third day of my captivity, the shooting stopped shortly before the first hint of light seeped into my room. My sleeping pad was soaked with the blood and fluids that had drained from my wound during the night. Ants crawled all over the pad and covered the floor where my wound had dripped the afternoon before. I jumped up and shook out the pad, stomped the ants, and moved to the other side of the room. If I stayed in that building very much longer the ants posed a problem. I was afraid that the gore attracting them would not quench their hunger and that they would attack me in my sleep.

The heat increased as the day wore on, and my room became like an oven. The temperature must have been 120 degrees in that building, but hunger distracted me from the heat, and hunger quickly took second place to thirst.

It was Sunday, and I had not had anything to drink since before leaving camp with the convoy on Friday. I had not eaten since Thursday night. I knew I could go without eating, but I knew I couldn't go long without water. I knocked on the door and didn't hear anything. I knocked again, but still heard nothing. Perhaps all the tank fire during the night ran everyone off. There was no sign of activity outside, not even dogs barking.

At various times throughout the morning, I could hear helicopters and fighter jets streak by in the distance on their way toward Fallujah. The tank bombardment the night before had a quieting effect on the bird life in the area, and even the stray dogs refused to bark.

Around noon, I heard a Bradley vehicle run down the road, firing its gun every few minutes. I decided to take a chance. I looked through the window to see if there was a guard outside. Peering toward the corner of the building, I looked for cigarette smoke drifting in the air or any other clue that might indicate the presence of a guard. I didn't see anything suspicious. I pulled a board loose from the wall and tied my black-and-white blindfold to it. I held it out the window, hoping to flag the Bradley down. It didn't work, and the armored vehicle's engine and track noise faded off into the distance.

I sat on the pad for an hour more before hearing a noise behind the building. Standing to look through the window I saw a young boy appear, walking away down an alley between two buildings. I hoped he would come back my way, so I waited, watching at the window for some 20 minutes. The sound of footsteps coming down the alley grabbed my attention. It was the boy. I waited until he got close to the window, I hollered, "Hey. Water. I need water." He looked up, paused a second, then ran like a scared rabbit. He acted like he had seen a ghost. He ran wide open and scaled a concrete-block fence that was more than four feet tall. I was afraid I had messed up. I was scared he was going to bring everybody back, but I never saw him again.

It must have been around five in the afternoon when I realized dehydration was taking its toll. There was no moisture in my mouth, no spit; my eyes were so dry that they were crusted shut and I had to use a finger to pull my eyelids open. I doubted that I would be able to make it through the night. *Was their plan to leave me here to die of thirst?* I wondered.

I got down on my knees and prayed again:

God, I don't want to die here, I have a family. I want to go home to them. God, I am going to need some water; I am not going to survive without it. I am going to lay right here. If I die, then I die. This is all your will. I have no control. I haven't fulfilled much here, and I know in my lifetime I haven't been out fellowshipping and talking to you. I have a lovely wife at home. My family is at home. I know they are going to be devastated if I die here. Whatever your will, I am fine with whatever it is. If I am to die here, then I am ready to die here.

I lay down with the full understanding that I would probably die right there in that position, on that pad.

Just a little after sundown a vehicle pulled up. Two pairs of sandals slapped the pathway. Someone put the key in the door and swung it open. Two men entered the room. I had not seen either one of the men before.

They ordered me to get up, took me outside, and pushed me into the same car. We drove back to the same building where we had shot the videotape. We walked through the room where we did the taping and into the next room. I sat down on the floor. Though I was in critical need of water, I did not ask for any. I did not want to beg for anything from the people who held me. If they were going to give me the water, they were going to have to offer it on their own.

As usual, the house was full of people milling around, talking among themselves. One of the men came over and asked if I wanted anything. I said, "Water." He brought two glasses of water and some cookies. I drank the water and ate the handful of sweet, tea-biscuit-type cookies. That was my first bite of food since I had been captured. After the cookies and water were gone he said he had somebody that he wanted me to talk with.

"You want me to talk to someone?" I said in disbelief. I figured they would bring one of their people to me, instead he told me to get up. We walked into another room. There was a man lying on the floor. His right leg was bandaged with gauze and supported by wooden splints made from 2-by-2 lumber. His leg was obviously broken around the knee area because his foot was turned 90 degrees in the wrong direction. He was not Arabic, probably from India or Pakistan, and he was wailing hysterically like a crazy man.

"He thinks we are going to kill him," said another man I had not seen before. "We want you to talk to him."

This other hostage was not helping his situation by crying and acting so upset. I sat down beside him. Everybody came into the room and gathered around us. "Are you married, do you have children?" I asked the bewildered man.

"Yes, I have a wife and children," he sputtered through tears.

"Good. You are a family man like me," I continued. "I talked to my God, I said, 'God you are going to have to take care of all of this.' I put it all in his hands. And I am not going to worry about it. I am not going to cry about this. You are going to have to calm down. You are hurt; you are going to have to calm down. They told me they are not going to harm you. They are not going to kill you. I am going to take them at their word." We just sat there quietly for a while. He stopped crying and settled down a bit.

He told me his name was Luga. I didn't want to get into a deep conversation with the man because I feared that our captors would interrogate me about what he might know. Our captors were certainly pleased with themselves about their selection of nourishment, because they kept shoving cookies at Luga and me.

The man who picked me up the day of the attack was sitting next to me. He pointed to my wedding ring. I knew he wanted it, and there was nothing I could do but let him take it. I hadn't taken the ring off in at least 10 years and was not sure it would come off. He grabbed it and started pulling, but the ring would not go over the knuckle. I said nothing to him. He kept trying to pull it off, but it would not come off. He stood there scowling, staring at my hand while he pondered how to remove the ring. I hoped he didn't want to cut off my finger just to steal it. More determined, he grabbed my hand again and resumed his tug-of-war. Finally, it popped off, and he stood there for a moment with a satisfied smirk.

As he strode across the room with his spoils, another man in the room pointed to him and said, "Tiger with women. He is Tiger. Tiger!" Well, Tiger may have stolen the hearts of Iraqi women, but he had just stolen my wedding ring. I was angry, but I didn't let it show.

When your total existence is focused on survival, the simplest things in life become the most important. Eating all of those cookies gave me stomach cramps. I needed to go to the bathroom. I did not know how to explain to them what I needed to do. I said the words "bathroom" and "toilet." One of the men mocked as if he was pulling down his pants and sitting on the toilet. I said, "YES!"

One of them said, "To-wallet, to-wallet." Another called it "W.C." Tiger mocked and chided me. I called it "to-wallet" from that point on. They walked outside and looked around to make sure no one was watching, certainly from the standpoint of secrecy rather than modesty. They then walked me outside to an outhouse, just like those we used in the old days in Mississippi, but unlike the two-hole bench seat we had growing up, there was just an indention in the floor, a small hole. Toilet paper is not used much in

Iraq, so when they handed me an urn filled with water; I knew what it was for. When in Rome, do as the Romans.

They walked me back inside, and we all sat down. At least 10 men, and possibly as many as 15, loomed throughout the house. Several of them wanted to talk and began firing questions at me.

"Why are you here?" one asked.

"Why's your country here?" another added.

"We are here to liberate your country, to bring you freedom," I responded.

"Saddam good, Saddam good," another faceless voice yelled.

"Glad he's gone," still another blasted back.

"Saddam good, good Saddam," argued another man.

Others in the room said they were glad he was gone. The mixture of opinions was confusing at the time, but would later become clear. The men, typically from cities, worked in Saddam's military and were unemployed. Reduced to living at the same impoverished level as the country folk (farmers), they were angered that their social status had been taken down a few notches. It was clear that the men were not all in agreement. They did agree on one point, though: they did not want Americans in Iraq.

After the discussion, I went back into the room with Luga for about an hour until they moved me to another room full of sleeping men. Instructed to lie down, I obeyed. This room full of men reminded me of the "Godfather" movies, when a Mafia family would gather in preparation for battle and "go to the mattresses." I guess my captors weren't worried about living up to their gangster counterparts in the movie. They settled for "going to the mats" instead. The only thing missing was the smell of cooking spaghetti.

I spent most of the night there and slept reasonably well, but it wasn't exactly a slumber party. Well before daylight, one of the men barked something in Arabic and motioned for me to get up. They took me outside to the same gray car. Blindfolded, I couldn't anticipate the movements of the car, so I swayed from side to side and had to lean on my handlers as we rounded curves.

We drove for about 40 minutes, the longest trip we had taken so far. They removed my blindfold as we stopped and parked the car at another house. It was dark, and the moon was shining bright as they walked me up to the small structure. The outline of a town marked the horizon. I heard a bird calling loudly. Its croaking call sounded like a water bird or crane, comparable to the calls of great blue herons found in the United States. I could smell "country." The musty odor of dirt and the sweet scent of evergreens filled the air. There were no "city" smells, no smoke stacks from refineries, oily asphalt, or smog stench. The familiar aroma of the country was comforting, and in a different situation would have been relaxing.

The building was a small, simple structure, like most of the others, and roughly 10 feet wide and 20 feet long. I cradled my drip bag as they led me inside. Even with nothing more than a kerosene lantern lighting the way, I could tell the furnishings were meager: a shelf with various spices for cooking and a box of powdered milk; a propane burner connected to a little 25-pound tank, similar to those we use back home at Southern fish fries; and a big clay pot on a stool, which seemed oddly out of place.

The men locked the door and left. I placed my sleeping pad next to the wall and lay on my left side so I could prop up my wounded right arm. I positioned the drip bag on my right hip. I was tired from having my sleep interrupted, so I easily drifted off to sleep.

It was a good thing I got some sleep during the day because sleep that night came hard. The mosquitoes were plentiful and hungry. I drifted off countless times, but in between one-armed battles against thirsty swarms of flying bloodsuckers, I managed only a few minutes of sleep.

Kellie, Tommy and Kellie's mother, Marla McEachern, at their wedding reception on July 9, 1987.

*Newlyweds Kellie and Tommy slice into
their wedding cake.*

SUNDAY,
APRIL 11, 2004
MACON, MISSISSIPPI

MORE THAN
YELLOW RIBBONS

In small towns like Macon, Mississippi, sense of community prevails. Like many other American hamlets, most of Macon's 2,410 residents know each other. When tragedy strikes, everyone rallies around those in need. When a native son was taken hostage, Macon was thrust into the international spotlight, and people took action. News spreads fast in small towns. The difference is that people rely on modern technology, not just the good ole cross-the-fence backyard network.

After news of Tommy Hamill's capture made its way around town and through the piney backwoods of Noxubee County, word spread that his family was pleading for prayers. That's all it took.

The day after the media reported that the hostage was

Tommy, the community went into action. Sunday, April 11 at dusk the first of many prayer vigils drew several hundred people. Every night a large group of residents from the city of Macon and the surrounding county gathered in front of the Noxubee County courthouse to pray for the safe return of one of their own. The weather had no effect on attendance. The community was there every night no matter what the climatic conditions. Folks from all walks of life joined the observance. Neither race nor religious affiliation mattered. The Macon masses became one unified family.

Giant yellow ribbons decorated the courthouse's six huge white columns, and the lights burned day and night as a beacon to guide Tommy home. The stately red brick structure became the central gathering spot for the citizens of the area. Around the town American flags flew on almost every home and business. Practically every vertical object in town wore a yellow bow. Signs requesting prayers for Tommy and his family dominated Jefferson Street.

The community didn't stop with the prayer vigils. "We never wanted for anything," Kellie said. "This community was absolutely amazing. They brought more food than we could eat. One of the convenience stores sent over mounds of barbecued pork with all the trimmings. Tems Food Mart got word to us that they would deliver anything we needed. The Junior Auxiliary brought over non-perishable items such as, laundry detergent, soft drinks, and snacks. A lady came and cleaned the house. Men just showed up to cut our grass. Several ladies from churches and the community, and even some members of the press, planted flowers around the house. A group of folks from all over the county arrived unannounced, power-washed and painted the exterior of our house.

"The Macon Fire Department hung a gigantic American flag from our roof. The Volunteer Fire Department planted a magnolia tree on May 1st at 8:30 in the morning in the front yard and tied yellow ribbons to its branches."

The way the community responded was akin to an old-fashioned barn raising back in the 1800s. Someone cried out for help and the people of Macon answered the call. The outpouring of kindness was endless. Though Kellie was locked up in her house, she knew what the community was doing. "We saw on TV all of the flags, ribbons, and signs," Kellie revealed. "The prayer vigil touched my heart in a powerful way. To know your neighbors are supporting you and praying for the same thing you are is simply moving. I cannot say enough about the good people of this community. Macon and this county showed their true colors."

*Both Tommy and Kellie are members of the Cedar Creek
Volunteer Fire Department. In 2003 Tommy was named
Noxubee County firefighter of the year.*

*Several hundred people gather on the lawn of the
Noxubee County courthouse for a prayer
vigil for Tommy's safe return.*

Seated in the wheelchair, Tommy's grandmother, Vera Hamill, attends one of the many functions honoring her grandson. Tommy's Aunt Coleene Higginbotham stands behind Mrs. Hamill with Melanie Thomas to her left.

**CHAPTER
8**

TUESDAY,
APRIL 13, 2004
IRAQ

THREE STOOGES TAKE THE STAGE

The morning of my fifth day of captivity a new group of four men took over as my guardians. Each sauntered in and began sizing me up, pacing back and forth, glancing at me over one shoulder then the other. One man carried an AK-47 but did not point it in my direction.

They brought in a breakfast of sliced cucumbers, cut lengthwise, and sliced tomatoes. The man wearing a purple headdress asked if I wanted some milk. I said I did. He asked if I wanted it hot or cold, I said hot. He lit the burner on the "fish fryer," boiled some water, and mixed up the powdered milk. I finished my first "meal" since being captured. Though we did not communicate much at first, the four men seemed to be more accommodating and caring than any of the others I had been with. Nevertheless, they were my guards, and I had to respect that.

The men were all in their late 20s to mid-30s. Three of them were about my height, five feet, nine inches tall, and the other was much taller, probably six feet, five inches tall. One of the guys, who appeared to be about 28 years old, was mostly bald-headed, and he acted silly and crazy from the time he walked in the door. He seemed on the verge of a breakdown. His voice was high pitched, and he usually spoke in a loud tone. He had a much lighter complexion than the other three and was a tad heavier. He was clean-shaven, but wore a thin, closely trimmed mustache. Because of the way he appeared and acted I decided to secretly nickname him "Curly," after one of the characters from "The Three Stooges." He probably tipped the scales a bit over 200 pounds. Curly wore a red headdress with a white robe, but did not wear his headdress on his head. It simply hung loose around his neck, and each end dangled at his waist.

Two of the others also fit the Three Stooges' profile. I named one "Larry" because of his kinky, unruly hair. He was quiet, with a very dark complexion, and wore a full beard. He wore "regular" clothes: dark pants, black loafers and socks, and a mid-tone shirt. He did not wear a headdress at all.

The third guy seemed a little more intelligent, more in control. If they had a leader, he was it. I named him "Moe." He told me later he was 28 years old. He, too, was clean-shaven, except for his closely trimmed mustache, and he talked more than the others. Moe wore a purple, plum-colored headdress and a tan robe. He likely weighed 25 to 30 pounds less than I did, putting him around 170 to 175.

The fourth guy, the one with the gun, had a very dark complexion. He walked slumped over, but still stood about six feet, five inches tall. I guess he was conditioned to walking hunched over after whacking his head on the low doorways common in Iraqi houses. A subdued, serious man, he stayed back from the other three — at times he was out of sight completely. The guy never looked right carrying a gun. He just did not look like the type of person who could shoot somebody. I called him "The Quiet One." He wore a white robe but did not put on a headdress.

I certainly did not consider any of them to be similar to the bumbling buffoons The Three Stooges portrayed in their act, though each of them — Moe, Larry, Curly, and The Quiet One — acted irrational at times. The names I had given them were simply for my own amusement.

Moe motioned for me to follow him outside. He gently gripped the bicep of my left arm and guided me away from the building. The man with the gun joined us as we crossed a ditch and went into some bushes. They stopped and handed me a water pitcher. The man with the gun motioned with his arm for me to continue into the bushes. I thought back to orientation with KBR when they warned us about deadly vipers. I watched each step to make sure there were no snakes camouflaged on the ground. Luckily none were lying in wait.

I was still wearing my Wrangler blue jeans from the morning of the attack. The jeans had grown stiff with dried blood. I had trouble pulling them down and could not button them up because there was no strength in my right-hand fingers. I managed to get my jeans back up, leaving the top button undone.

We went back inside. One of the men asked if I wanted my clothes cleaned, and I nodded yes. They pulled my pants and shirt off and handed me a one-piece white *dishdasha* robe. It felt a little strange wearing a dress, but it sure was easier to manage, especially when going to the bathroom.

Shortly, they blindfolded me and situated me in a small off-white color car. We drove about two miles when I felt the car tilt upward to climb a small hill then level off as we stopped in the carport of a new location. Moe said that this was where they lived. I remained blindfolded as we went inside. Air swirled overhead as they removed my blindfold. The men left me in a room that was about 20 feet wide and 40 feet long. There was no furniture, only those small, thin sleeping pads encircling the floor. Exposed wires, tacked to the walls, ran from a speed control box up to two wobbling ceiling fans. It looked like that room was their sleeping quarters with thin pads placed around the floor's edge. From what I could see, the rest of the house looked nice and well appointed with nice curtains and a decorative wall clock. A photograph of a man who looked to be a priest hung on the far wall.

A couple of young kids were playing loudly outside. Soon, one began to cry at the top of his voice as if he'd been hurt. The lights from a TV, set to an Arabic channel, flickered on the other side of a pair of double doors.

In a little while, they came back into the room with another man I had not seen before. He was dressed in typical American-style clothes: pressed black pants, black penny-loafer shoes, and a dark gray, cotton shirt. Moe kept saying, "Doctor. Doctor. He is a doctor." I still had the IV attached to my left arm, though it was not functioning very well. Blood had backed up in the line, and with very little liquid remaining, the bag was barely dripping.

The doctor entered the room talking in two different languages. He would start speaking in English then out of the blue switch over to Arabic then back to broken English. He was trying to explain what he was doing, but I did not understand him. He removed the IV from my arm, unwrapped my wound, cleaned it with peroxide and iodine, then re-bandaged it. There was just a tiny strip of skin holding the flap of muscle in place, but I knew the muscle would soon die because it was not getting enough blood to stay alive. Cleaning it with peroxide and iodine was not going to prevent infection. I also realized that infection could not only cause me to lose my arm but also could take my life.

Even with that knowledge, I felt a complete peace about me. I had turned the whole situation over to God and felt He would take care of me.

The doctor prepared an array of medical supplies, such as individually wrapped syringes, cotton balls, vials of saline, gauze, and Ace bandages, and placed them into a large yellow plastic bag and two smaller bags, which were about the size of a typical Wal-Mart bag. He set a gallon jug of iodine and a bottle of hydrogen peroxide in a cardboard box.

The doctor called Moe over and gave him a quick rundown of the supplies and instructions for their use. Moe appeared to understand, and he set the bags next to the door.

Before the doctor left me, he inserted another IV, this one into a vein in my left hand for the purpose of administering antibiotics twice daily. I no longer had the drip bag to carry around. He administered the first dose through the new IV.

I tried to explain to the doctor that I was on a daily seizure medication of 400 mg of Dilantin. I was concerned I might have a seizure and my captors wouldn't understand. I asked the doctor if he could get some Dilantin for me, but he never did.

I stayed there the rest of the day. When night fell, Moe blindfolded me and drove me about two miles to a building I had not seen previously. Because of its shape, I named it the "L-shaped building." They left the medical supplies, cookies, plenty of bottled water, and an oil-burning lantern in the corner of the room. The car drove away. I did not know who was guarding the outside, but I could hear at least two voices.

A few mosquitoes swarmed throughout the night, but they weren't bad enough to keep me from sleeping reasonably well. I left the lantern burning until morning.

Chapter 9

Tuesday,
April 13, 2004
Macon, Mississippi

Hiding from the Media

A prisoner in her own home, Kellie Hamill didn't step outside for the first four days her husband was in captivity. "I
felt like I was being held hostage in my own home," she
said. "Members of the media have a job to do, but they
could give people some space. They shouldn't hold someone hostage in their home and hang around the front door
just to get a picture. They need to give a person time to
come to grips with what has happened before they bom-
bard them with cameras and questions."

To protect their friends, Doris and Jesse took off work
to stay with Kellie every day. Jesse became the family's
media shield and placed the necessary phone calls to find
out what was going on in Iraq. "Jesse had to use his cell
phone to make calls, because we could not get a line out

at my house," Kellie said. "Almost every time one of us picked up the phone there would be a media person on the other end. We couldn't even get a dial tone. I couldn't talk to my father every day like I wanted because I couldn't call out, and the line was busy when he tried to call. We could not even take a call without the second line beeping in. I was scared to not answer the beep because it might have been KBR or even Tommy trying to call. It terrified me not to answer the phone. I was afraid Tommy did not remember my cell phone number, so I wanted to keep the phone line at the house clear. Tommy was going through the worst ordeal of his life, but so was I. The wondering, not knowing, and the hassle were torture."

People from all over the world called to lend encouragement. "The wives of other KBR employees called to lend their support," Kellie said. "I appreciated each and every one of their calls. Without the prayers of the community, the nation, and all of the individuals, we would not have pulled through this. On the other hand, I just wanted the phone to quit ringing. I was so fearful that Tommy would try to call and not be able to get through. The media called up until midnight. I got calls at three and four in the morning, mostly from folks at Camp Anaconda. I never turned down a phone call."

The media camped on the road adjacent to the Hamill house. Without Kellie, they settled for playing with the dogs and shooting footage of everything in sight. ABC, NBC, FOX, Louis Bailey with Sharpshooter Worldwide, and all the local affiliates from Jackson, Columbus,

Meridian, West Point, Mississippi, and many others clogged the road.

"Before I could face all of those people I had to get myself together," Kellie said. "I didn't want to get on camera and lose it or show fear. If I did, it might make it harder on Tommy. If somehow Tommy saw me on TV, I didn't want him to see fear in my eyes or see me cry. The media asked me how I was so strong. It wasn't that I was strong; they just weren't going to see a side of me I didn't want to show. The media can eat you alive or they can be your friends. Fortunately, there were a few people in the media who were good to us and honest in their approach."

*Seated in her living room, Kellie Hamill makes
her first public statement to the press
after news of Tommy's capture.*

CHAPTER
10

WEDNESDAY,
APRIL 14, 2004
IRAQ

THREE MEALS AND SHAAY

As I awakened at sunrise there was just enough light passing through the window and door transom to allow me to study the details of the room in the L-shaped building. It was made of masonry blocks and covered with a thin coating of tan-colored grout. Heavy iron bars, mounted on the exterior, fortified a rear window, which was about three feet wide and four feet tall.

The entry door was metal with a deadbolt lock and a short glass transom mounted above. The transom's glass was divided in half by a vertical angle-iron bar. It flashed in my mind that it might be possible to knock out the angle iron and crawl head first through the opening, but it would have been tight. The more I thought about it, the more I realized it would be next to impossible to get up that high and pull myself with just one good arm. I did manage to jump up, grab the transom sill, and pull myself up just high enough to take a quick look outside. Moe and the men had tried to cover the window with tree limbs, leaves, and grass, but I could still see through the tiny spaces in the vegetation. The bars on the rear window would be impossible to break through for an escape.

The ceiling was about 12 to 14 feet high. The dirt floor was virtually hard as concrete and had tiny potholes where a leaky roof had pitted the earth. An electrical line ran from the top of the wall to an empty white porcelain light socket, which was mounted head high on the side of the wall. That was the only sign of electricity in the room. The night's illumination came from a single oil lantern.

About eight in the morning on the sixth day of captivity, a car pulled up and two doors slammed. Moe, Larry, Curly, and The Quiet One shuffled in, speaking Arabic to each other. Soon, Moe and Larry blindfolded me and walked me outside to use the bathroom. The small room, or short leg of the "L" shape, was probably once used as a stable but had since become the "bathroom." We had to go outside and enter an exterior door to gain entrance into the crude latrine. The "commode" was no more than a shallow hole in the dirt floor.

We walked back inside, and Moe took hold of my right wrist and drew it closer to his face to examine my bandage, which was wet from draining during the night. He began to peel the bandage from the wound. The gauze was stuck to the skin and hurt a little as he ripped it away.

The site was beginning to look infected. The edges around the wound were puffy, yellowish pus oozed from under the dead flap of muscle, and some of the tissue had green edges. The wound emitted a sweet, sick smell similar to meat that is just beginning to go bad.

Moe rummaged around in the yellow plastic bag the doctor had given him and pulled out the gauze and Ace bandages. The doctor must have given him lessons in first aid as he quickly rewrapped the wound. He then squirted the vial of liquid into a container of the powder, shook it up, pulled it into the syringe, and injected it into the IV in my hand.

"Are you a Christian," as he signed the cross, "or Islamic, Muslim?" Moe asked matter-of-factly.

"I am a Christian." I answered without hesitation. That answer seemed to satisfy him; at least it suited him for the time being.

They brought breakfast in on a tarnished silver aluminum platter and set it between us on the floor. There was, what appeared to be, clabbered milk in a pan sitting in the middle of the platter. It looked like milk that had been in the refrigerator 20 days beyond the expiration date. The watery stuff had the consistency of cottage cheese but with irregular lumps. Next to the milky goop was a stack of leaven bread called *hubis* which is traditional Iraqi flat bread made with flour, yeast, and water. I wasn't sure how I was supposed to eat my meal.

They motioned for me to eat, so I tore off a strip of bread and dipped it in the thick, watery substance. I looked up for approval. The men gave no indication as to whether or not I was eating it incorrectly, so I continued to lightly dip the bread as they watched. It wasn't bad, but they didn't eat. The meal had a sweet-and-sour taste. I prayed to myself as I ate,

God, I don't know what they may have done to this food. If they have done anything to this food you are going to have to take care of it. I have to eat to survive. I am going to eat this food regardless. If they have done something, you will have to keep it from harming me.

After breakfast Moe said to me, "Walk," as he wiggled two fingers back and forth. My only exercise until then had been walking to the outhouse and going back and forth to the car. I walked from one wall to another for about 10 minutes. It was just enough to loosen me up and work out some of the stiffness that had set in over the past week.

Curly and The Quiet One left soon after breakfast, marking the first of many "shift changes." Moe and Larry went outside and stayed until the other two returned with lunch; they were determined to keep me fed. They brought rice, stewed tomatoes, flat bread, and water. Again they placed the tray between us, only this time they ate as well. I wasn't sure how to eat that fare either. Moe poured two spoonfuls of the stewed tomatoes onto the rice and began eating with his spoon from the bowl of rice, I did likewise. I ate from one side of the bowl, and they ate from the other. I studied Moe as he tore off a piece of bread, cupped it, and then scooped some of the tomatoes, like dipping chips in salsa. I followed suit. The food was full of flavorful spices. The rice was seasoned with a variety of spices, but none of the food was too hot to enjoy. There was more chow than all five of us could eat. For the first time since being captured, I had breakfast and lunch on the same day.

They left the room shortly after lunch to assume their guard stations outside the door. I spent many hours alone, but never felt lonely. I had a peace and calm that can only come with faith and trust in God. I briefly thought about Kellie, Thomas, and Tori and wondered how they were dealing with the uncertainty. I asked the Lord to give me strength not to dwell on thoughts of my family. I did not want those thoughts to turn into frustration causing me to do something stupid that might get me killed.

I was concerned about the men in my convoy who may have been captured as well. Most of them had not been there very long; several had only been there for a month. I thought, *If they show fear or are so afraid that they don't eat the food they are given, the bad guys will see that as disrespect. If they continue to be afraid, those guys are going to eat them up. You have got to stand up to these people.*

Why am I not afraid? I asked myself. *This is not like me. When I first came over here I was afraid of being shot, being burned.* My worst fear was being burned alive in a truck. KBR had trucks blown up and people killed in convoys. I had been afraid of going to Iraq. I had experienced fear at different times in my life, but God took all of the fear away from me from the beginning of my captivity.

The window was the main source of light for the room and my only view of the world outside. I dragged my pad and pillows and placed them under the window, close to the wall. There was a concrete masonry block in the room that I turned up lengthwise, set it up against the wall, and used it as a stool. I would lean it against the wall underneath the window and sit on the block. I spent many hours peering through the bars on that window.

Moe came into the room about midafternoon carrying a homemade mat made of palm leaves. He spread it on the floor, knelt down on it, and began to pray aloud in Arabic. The prayer lasted a couple of minutes. He then rolled the mat up and walked back outside. A while later Larry came in with his mat and prayed in the same manner.

I was surprised when they showed up with dinner. It looked like enough food to feed six people: a bowl full of rice, lots of bread, an okra-based soup, stewed tomatoes, and only one bottle of water. They sat down with me and we all began to eat. One of the men took a drink from the water bottle and handed it to me. Without hesitation, I took a drink and handed it to the other man. I did not want to insult them by refusing to drink after them. I did not wipe the top of the bottle off before I drank. I showed them respect.

I tried to eat as much as I could. They insisted I eat more and I tried to accommodate, but there was more food than I could eat. There was always food left over, which they may have fed to members of their family. They made sure I did not get hungry, and always left at least two packages of tea-biscuit cookies for between-meal snacks.

Conversation with my captors took quite a bit of time. They talked very slowly. Where it might take me a second or two to drawl out a few words, it took them ten times as long. If I spoke at my normal rate, they could not understand anything. Before they could say a word, they would have to think about its pronunciation, and then try articulating it in English. Each word had to be thought out before they attempted to utter its sound.

After we finished Curly said, "Whiskey, you want?"

"Naw, no whiskey, I don't drink. No whiskey."

"*Shaay? Shaay?*" he asked then.

I shrugged my shoulders, not knowing what he meant.

They left, but returned soon with a steaming kettle wrapped in a towel. One of them filled a glass, not much larger than a shot glass, half full of sugar and then topped it off with what looked to be tea. The leaves slowly swirled in the brown-tinted water. Even though I am accustomed to tea without the flotsam, I drank it and it was good.

"*Shaay?*" I asked holding up the glass.

"Yes, *shaay.*"

"It's good," I concluded.

They brought tea from then on, after every meal. No matter how many glasses I drank, they would always ask if I wanted one more.

That was the beginning of a routine of three meals a day. Like clockwork, at the same time every day, they brought more food than I could possibly eat. Though I did not have a watch, I knew within minutes when the food would arrive. All the food and unlimited water helped build my strength and re-hydrate my body. The infection in my arm, however, was taking its toll on my strength and made me sleepy at times.

After the meal and tea, Moe mixed up the antibiotic formula and injected it into the IV catheter. There was no indication the medicine was working, but it was only the second day of treatment.

Before leaving, Larry refilled the lantern with oil, lit it with a match, and set it in the corner. I managed to sleep off and on that night. The temperature cooled off, probably dropping down into the mid-50s, which made it easier to sleep for longer periods of time.

CHAPTER

11

THURSDAY,
APRIL 15, 2004
IRAQ

FIRST BATH

The day before, the wound on my arm smelled a little rank, but by the morning of my seventh day in captivity the stench had grown much stronger. It smelled like rotting road kill. The flap of muscle and the flesh beneath decayed more each day. Around the edges, the hole in my arm was black and tough as leather; in the middle, the wound oozed with pus. It drained so much the bandage stayed soaking wet. I could feel it bubbling, boiling underneath the bandage. There was no doubt it was reaching the critical stage. But as bad as the infected wound looked, I had experienced no pain.

Breakfast arrived with Moe and Larry at the same time as the pervious day. The menu was the same as the morning before. All four men joined me, but before we started Curly made the sign of the cross and asked, "Are you a Christian, or Islamic, Muslim?" That would become the

114

question every morning to start the day.

"I am a Christian," I said.

"Where does America have Saddam?" Curly asked in his shrill voice.

"I have no idea," I countered.

"President Bush. Saddam. Whiskey. Both of them (are) somewhere drinking whiskey together."

"Naw, I don't think so," I said, hoping that discussion would end with that.

Curly perked up more and at the top of his voice said, "Yes, yes, President Bush and Saddam, whiskey, they drink whiskey together."

"Yeah, right," I snorted sarcastically.

That conversation went nowhere; it didn't even make sense. I turned my attention to the business of eating. I silently hoped Curly would not want to engage me in another chat. As soon as we finished our meal I was blindfolded by Moe, and we all rode the two miles or so to the doctor's home.

Three men were sitting on the floor when we entered. One looked like a cleric, minister, or holy man of some degree. He wore a nice pressed white *dishdasha* robe and a square, flat brimless white hat. Moe said the other two were surgeons. They sat me down next to the three men. One removed the bandage from my arm. The smell was putrid. They examined the wound, cleaned it, and wrapped it back up. I just shook my head. The treatment I was receiving was not adequate. I thought, *If God does not intervene, I am not going to live through this.*

The Quiet One asked if I needed to wash. It was Thursday afternoon, and I had not bathed since Friday morning. Surely they noticed. "Yes, I would like a bath," I said, thinking they might have a shower in the doctor's house.

The Quiet One blindfolded me and walked me out the door. We took a right, then another right. We walked down a gentle slope and followed a furrowed pathway down a little hill, made a left turn, and crossed a small ditch where I could feel clumps of grass under my feet. We turned right and walked straight to an outhouse. Larry tagged along sloshing a pan of warm water all the way.

The Quiet One instructed me to remove the *dishdasha* robe. I was aware Iraqi men did not like seeing other men naked, so I left on my boxer briefs. I stood there not knowing what would come next. He began tossing water over my body to get me wet. I was taken aback when he started washing my hair. He rinsed out the soap and proceeded to wash my arms and back. He cupped his hand, turned upward, and motioned for me to do the same. He filled my palm with granulated soap, then added a little water, and pointed to my groin area. Leaving my underwear on, I washed as best I could.

He poured water over me to rinse off the soap. They had brought a pair of gray jersey-cloth sweatpants and a black short-sleeved sweat top. I felt so refreshed; my skin was clean and breathing again.

Larry and The Quiet One drove me back to the L-shaped building where we soon had our usual fare for lunch. I figured the meals were prepared at the doctor's house and transported to the L-shaped building. All three of us stuffed ourselves again. They went outside to resume whatever they did out there.

I had been having trouble with the IV catheter in my hand bending over backwards and nearly working itself out. Aggravation set in and I jerked it out.

Larry entered the room about midafternoon carrying his homemade mat made of palm leaves. He spread it on the floor, knelt down on it, and began to pray aloud in Arabic. The prayer sounded similar to the one he said aloud the day before. He then rounded the mat up and went back outside. They seemed to have no reservations about expressing their faith in front of me nor did they have any qualms about discussing it with me. I felt the same way. I did not cover the fact I am a Christian and told them so at every opportunity.

The L-shaped building was located on the edge of the desert, and when peering through the window, I could see for a long distance. Directly behind the building was a small irrigation system that sprayed water over a miniature truck farm garden. The rest of the ground looked hard with scattered patches of grass. To the right was a large fallow agricultural field with a huge center-pivot irrigation system, which was not completely assembled; the wheels had not been installed. The frame was painted red and had the company name inscribed in French on the side. I could read the word "FranceCo" as the company's name. There were similar irrigation systems all over Iraq, used primarily to water the wheat fields. I spent much of the afternoon looking out that window.

Moe and Curly returned a while later with dinner. It was pretty much the same food each time, with the alternates of sliced cucumbers, tomatoes, or okra soup. All four men ate with me. As always, there was plenty of *shaay* after the meal. I drank three glasses of the sweetened tea.

Moe noticed I no longer had the IV in my hand and asked what had happened. I demonstrated that it had worked itself almost out and that I finished the job. He thought for a minute, then went to the yellow plastic bag, took out a syringe of powder and the saline vial, and promptly mixed and shook it. He pointed to his hip then to mine. I lowered my sweatpants and underwear. Moe popped me good and forced the medicine in a little too fast. It burned and stung quite a bit.

They also had brought a low-wattage light bulb. They screwed it into the fixture on the wall. Its strength of illumination varied. It would burn bright for a while, go dim for a few seconds, and then go out completely for an hour. I was not sure of the electricity source, but I could hear a generator in the distance and figured that was it.

Moe and Larry left for the night, and Curly and The Quiet One stood watch outside. I could hear them talking from time to time for a couple of hours just outside the door. The temperature cooled by as much as 50 degrees at night, which was comfortable and allowed me to sleep.

*Concrete irrigation canals and ditches crisscross the arid
ground within reach of Iraq's Tigris and Euphrates Rivers,
enabling local farmers to produce crops.*

Chapter
12

Friday,
April 16, 2004
Iraq

The Doctor Makes House Calls

As the morning light crept into my cell on the eighth day of captivity, I spied four lizards hanging around the light bulb. I had a hard time spotting the little rascals, because they were the same color as the wall. They hung around the light and found easy meals by catching insects that were attracted to the glow of the bulb.

The lizards would crawl real close to me then run away. I didn't know if they were a poisonous variety or not. They reminded me of the fence swifts we have back home. One of them darted toward me, and I instinctively grabbed my sandal and hit it, killing it. It was an impulsive reaction, one I later regretted.

Moe and Larry arrived on time with breakfast. All four

men came into the room. Moe and Curly propped their weapons next to the wall and sat down for our usual meal of clabbered milk, leaven bread, water, and *shaay*.

"Are you a Christian or Islamic, Muslim?" Moe asked as he motioned the Catholic sign of the cross.

"I am a Christian," I repeated. The days were becoming routine, the question about my faith, the march to the bathroom, the changing of the guard, the three meals, and my gazing out the window.

Moe took a quick look at my arm and decided not to change the bandage. He mixed the liquid and powder in the syringe and injected it into my hip.

Then Moe looked up at me with a serious expression and, using his hands to communicate, placed his fingers underneath his eyes and slowly raked them down his cheeks. He repeated the act three times and said, "Your family cries for you. We see on television." I didn't know what effect, if any, the sight of my family crying would have on my captors, or if he was even telling the truth. There was no need to react in an anxious or overjoyed way. But if he was telling the truth, I at least knew my family was alive and well.

Curly and The Quiet One went outside. Moe signaled for me to exercise, so I walked from one wall to the other for 10 minutes. About midmorning, Moe came in and knelt on his mat for prayer. A few minutes after he left Larry came in and did likewise.

Time passed quickly between breakfast and lunch. When Moe and Larry returned, we sat down to our standard fare of rice, cucumbers, stewed tomatoes, bread, water, and *shaay*. They insisted that I eat large portions, and I obliged, so much so that I was often not very hungry when they arrived with the next meal. Though lunch was tasty, I had to choke down the last few bites.

Moe examined my bandage again, finding it soaked with the fluid that was draining from my arm. It was getting worse by the day. Without hesitation he began the painful process of unwrapping and stripping away the embedded gauze. It was so embedded in the wound that he had to pour iodine over the gauze to liquefy the dried blood. That trick worked only moderately well, but the bandage eventually came off. He wrapped fresh gauze over the smelly site. With his nursing care completed, Moe picked up his weapon and took Larry with him, leaving Curly and The Quiet One outside to guard the building.

I spent that afternoon peeping through the maze of plant life covering the window. All of the French-made irrigation systems in the fields beyond the window got me to wondering if maybe the trade of products and services had something to do with the French not wanting to support the United States in the conflict. Iraq may have owed France for those systems and other products, and perhaps the French were concerned about getting paid or not being able to do business with Iraq in the future.

Again Moe and Larry entered the room to kneel and pray. That was the first time I had seen them pray twice in one day. I had thought they prayed at the same time every day.

Curly and The Quiet One arrived with dinner between 7 and 8 o'clock. Curly was as peppy as ever, "Mister, mister. How are you today, mister?"

"I'm fine," I said.

Moe leaned his gun against the wall and everyone gathered around and began adding the stewed tomatoes to the rice, taking bits of cucumbers, and scooping the rice mixture with leaven bread. By that time I knew the drill and ate as they did as if I'd been doing it for a lifetime.

After dinner Curly rubbed an iodine-soaked cotton ball on my upper left hip and gave me an antibiotic shot. He injected the solution way too fast causing it to burn like liquid fire. I tried telling him he was squeezing the syringe too fast. He didn't understand and merely instructed me to rub the site to stop the burning.

Moe and Larry left, and Curly and The Quiet One went outside. Later that night, around 11 o'clock, the doctor and Moe showed up unexpectedly. Moe told me to get up and said, "Go see doctors." He blindfolded me, as they always did anytime we left the building, and walked me to the car. They did not say why or where we were going, only that we were going to see doctors. I didn't ask questions.

We drove for 45 to 60 minutes. I could always wiggle, twitch my face, then tilt my head back a little, and see underneath the blindfold. City lights flickered in the open space ahead; I thought we might be close to Baghdad. We crossed a couple of bridges and turned onto a dirt road. I soon heard the crunching of gravel under the car's wheels.

We drove five or six minutes more then pulled up to an

old house around midnight. Though the house was run down, a family lived there. The windows were barred but had no glass or curtains. We made our way inside where pads lay spread on the floor. I figured they were just relocating me again. After all, I had been at the L-shaped building longer than at any other place.

The two doctors who had examined my arm the day before drifted in. Both men described themselves as surgeons. One was the lead surgeon, while the other mostly assisted and observed. The assistant carried a small, flat, stainless steel pan, which held a scalpel and other surgical instruments. We all sat on the floor. I watched as the surgeon poured iodine over their utensils. The surgeon sat on my right side, while the assistant sat on my left. They had a large stainless steel bowl they used as an operating table. The surgeon had me place my arm down into the bowl and turn my hand so the wound was exposed to him. I felt no pain at all.

A group of onlookers drifted into the room and just squatted there to watch the procedure. One of them, who had his face wrapped to where only his eyes showed, stared at me with a distant look as if he was glaring completely through me. Another guy spoke out, "Are you afraid? Are you afraid of what they are going to do?"

"No, I am not afraid. I know this has to happen. I am not afraid."

"You mean you are not afraid of what he is going to cut on your arm?"

"No, I am not afraid," I said in a firmer voice. "I have

put this in God's hands. He has control over all of this. Whatever they are doing, He's got his hands in it with them. I am not afraid of anything."

Two men had their faces fully cloaked with a scarf. All I could see were their eyes. A young boy, maybe 12 to 13 years old, loomed in the background. He appeared to be just a little younger than my son, Thomas.

The doctors began explaining what they were going to do to me. The surgeon said, "We have a lot of dead tissue here that we are going to have to cut away. We have to get down to the good muscle tissue."

I didn't know what they were going to cut when they started slicing with that scalpel.

"We are going to give you a local anesthetic."

The doctor filled a syringe and tried injecting the medicine, but the needle wouldn't penetrate; the skin around the edge of the wound had hardened and turned black. He carefully worked the needle into the skin around the edge of the wound six or seven times and once right in the middle of it. I watched his every move.

The surgeon started cutting away. I kept watching as he whacked off the big flap of rotten muscle tissue. Then they pulled out two pieces of bone fragments. The other doctor, the assistant, kept saying, "Look away. Look the other direction. Why are you watching?"

I was amazed, privileged in a sense, to be able to watch something like that.

He wouldn't let up, "You need to look away, don't look at that."

"But, I'm not afraid to look."

In an effort to distract me he asked, "Why is America here, why do you come to Iraq?"

I gave him the short answer, "We are here to liberate your country, to bring freedom to the Iraqi people."

I kept my attention on the surgeon as he finished his work. He said, "We are going to have to... we didn't get all of the dead tissue. There will be more that will die after this. We are going to have to come back on a follow-up. But this is all we are going to do now."

The crowd of shrouded spectators left the room.

He went on as if he was trying to sell me on the ability of the Iraqi medical-care system. "We can fix the bone, we can do that. We can do skin grafts here. We've got the technology here to do everything to this arm. We can't do that now because they (my captors) don't want you to go to a hospital. We can save your arm here, without going to the hospital. You can have skin and bone grafts done later. According to Islam we cannot reconstruct the bone and skin. You are a prisoner, and we can only help fix what is threatening your life."

I wondered if they thought I was going to be released soon and could get the grafting done when I got home. I took it as a positive sign.

The doctor to my left, the assistant who talked to me a lot, asked if I wanted him to send an e-mail to my wife. I knew they had my e-mail address, because it was in my wallet. I simply told them to tell my family that I am doing fine, that they (the Iraqis) are doing surgery to my arm. As far as

I know he never sent it.

I thought I was going to stay there for the night. A man, unknown to me, fixed up a pad and blanket, and I laid down for 30 minutes or so. They came right back and said we were moving. Blindfolded, I was driven a couple of miles down the road to yet another small house. It was somewhere around 1:30 or 2:00 in the morning at that point. We entered a small room in the house. The only thing in the room was a bullet-riddled refrigerator. They brought a pad in, helped me lay down, and left the room leaving the lights on.

I lay there with my eyes partially closed as a TV blared away in the next room. Four or five young teenage boys strolled through the room and stopped periodically to look at me. I watched them through my eyelashes as they studied me and whispered to each other. A man who was there when we arrived walked into the room, clutched one of the boys, and walked over to me. I sat up. "This is this boy's father's home," he said. "American soldiers came here one night, shot up the house, and took him. He is a prisoner now." He turned and walked away.

I lay there for 15 to 20 minutes. Another unknown man came in and ordered me up and escorted me into the next room. There were seven or eight men lying on pads all around the room watching a 19-inch television. It was obvious he had not told the men I was coming in, because one of the men, lying with his feet toward the TV, looked around at me and immediately started wrapping up his face. I recognized him as one of the two guys who wore the scarf covering his face during my surgery. I lay down on a pad next to him.

That pad was more comfortable than the others. It was about the thickness of a mattress and very soft. It took a lot of pressure off my back. The thin pads I had been lying on before offered no padding between my body and the hard clay floors.

No one talked as the man with the remote control kept flipping through the channels. We watched an Australian travel channel that showed fishing and canoeing in the Outback. They went through the Arab channels stopping occasionally. I was trying to catch one of the news channels, hoping to see something about my family or me. The masked man lying next to me offered a cigarette. I said, "No, I don't smoke. Smoking is bad for your health, bad for your health."

He lit a cigarette and smoked it through his wrap. He would pull the wrap apart to create an opening so he could draw on his cigarette. He'd draw, exhale, and then pull the cloth back over his lips.

I looked him straight in the eye and asked, "Are you one of the men who was involved in the attack on my convoy?"

He tried talking through his wrap. He did not want me to see his mouth. His voice was squeaky, high pitched. I could barely understand him. "I was in the attack on your convoy," he admitted.

I said, "I am not angry at you for this. I know I probably lost some men, but I'm not angry. This is war."

I felt led to talk with him, a man who had possibly killed some of my men. "America is here to help the Iraqi people," I said in a calm voice. "I wish you could understand that we are here to help. Can't you understand that people like Saddam and his sons didn't need to treat people like they did? We have freedoms in America. In America I can talk bad about our president if I don't like him. I can say anything I want about him. Here if you said anything bad about Saddam you would be killed or imprisoned. We are over here trying to help."

"Why do you bomb Fallujah?" he asked.

"You can kill me today," I said. "You can do me like you did the guys in Fallujah. Then President Bush is going to come in here and bomb more. Look, President Bush is trying to do this right. He does not want to kill the good people of Iraq, only the bad guys. If he wanted to, he could wipe Iraq off the map. There would be no more Iraq. We have the technology and the weaponry to do that and not put a single U.S. soldier on the ground. But we don't want to do that. Bush is trying to save Iraqi lives. American soldiers are paying the price for doing it this way."

"I understand," he said.

"Do you understand we are trying to help?" I followed.

"We don't want America here," he responded. "America just wants our oil. Let me ask you, who is president of Iraq?"

I thought a few seconds and answered, "Iraq does not have a president right now."

"Yes, Iraq does have president. President Bush. This

new government is puppet government of the United States. Bush bad, bad Bush."

"If you think Bush is bad, who do you think were good U.S. presidents?"

"President Clinton good. Good president, Clinton. Kennedy good. Eisenhower good. And Schwarzenegger good. Schwarzenegger good, good Schwarzenegger, he's good man."

I didn't bother telling him that Arnold Schwarzenegger was now governor of California. I am not sure how *The Terminator* was abruptly thrust into a discussion of U.S. presidents, but the masked man did speak about enjoying "Schwarzenegger's" movies.

I was trying to find out what it would take to stop the fighting. I switched gears and asked, "Can you control what's going on? This fighting has got to stop. Can you let them know; hey, we are stopping all of these attacks on this road? It is only a six-mile stretch of road. Can you stop it?"

"Yes, I can do that," he casually said.

"At this point we are just fighting," I explained. "There are no negotiations, no talks. There are no two people who can get together and talk about this. I see it as two people that are staring at each other. They are just one step away from shaking hands, talking this out, and stopping the fighting. Your people are going to continue to fight, and our soldiers are going to keep fighting. America needs a sign that you want to try to negotiate. Can you stop it?"

"I have the authority to do that. I can have that done," he said.

In a way, he acted like he would make the request to stop the attacks on the freeway. I don't know if the attacks slowed after that or not.

Our conversation was interrupted by a buzzing sound overhead. I knew what it meant. It was an unmanned aerial vehicle, also known as a drone. Then I heard the Apaches. Not far away, one opened fire. I stayed inside while all of the other men ran outside and started looking up. The drone kept flying back and forth.

I was afraid those guys were going to shoot at it. If they had fired a shot, the building where we hid would have been blown to smithereens.

The Apaches got close a couple of times, firing as they passed. They fired up and down the road. The helicopter's cannons fired sporadically for nearly an hour and then faded away. That was a close call; I was surprised we didn't become the target.

Sunrise was only a couple of hours away. The men filtered back into the room and began drifting off to sleep. With things relatively quiet, I finally dozed off for a couple of hours of much needed rest.

*Governor Arnold Schwarzenegger speaks to soldiers
before their departure for Iraq.*

An AH-64 Apache helicopter gunship.

SATURDAY,
APRIL 17, 2004
IRAQ

THE RAT
KILLIN'

The ninth day of my captivity began with everybody rising slowly and milling about the compound for a few minutes. The doctor and Moe tied a blindfold over my eyes, led me (thankfully) by my uninjured arm, and guided me to the doctor's car. Even blindfolded, I could see the sun rising above the horizon. I estimated the time to be about 9 o'clock.

We rode for 20 to 30 minutes and then stopped at yet another house. They led me into a large, long room. Moe walked into another room, and I did not see him again while I was there. There was an older man wearing a nice white *dishdasha* robe standing near a podium at the far end. I presumed the room was used for religious meetings.

They sat me down. A man wearing a dark tan robe, whom I had not seen before, asked if I wanted something to eat. I nodded yes, and he brought me more tea biscuits and a cup of hot milk. As I ate the cookies the man talked to me, "I was in Saddam's army for two years. I have four brothers and three sisters. My brothers were also in Saddam's army. Three of them are here. I want them to meet you. I will bring them in."

Two of the brothers entered the room wearing white robes. One of the men said he had been in Saddam's army for 10 years. The third brother, wearing a tan robe, walked in holding the hand of a pretty little girl who had a smooth, dark complexion, and beautiful long black hair. She was about three or four years old. He said she wanted to say hello to me. Smiling, she softly greeted me in Arabic. I said hello and returned her smile. Satisfied, she turned and walked away. I told her father that she was very beautiful.

An old woman, perhaps 80 years old, came into the room. The man introduced her as his mother. She knelt down on the floor in front of me and began praying aloud in Arabic. "She is praying for you," said her son. "She is praying they release you."

As they knelt they prayed to Allah, asking what my fate might be. They were asking for guidance from their god. They were not waiting for a judge or jury to hand down a verdict. They were waiting for an answer from Allah as to whether I would be killed or released.

The man was very curious and wanted to continue our discussion. He told me he believed, "In America a son is only a son until he is 18."

"That's right," I responded. "When you turn 18 you

make your own decisions. You're free to make your own mistakes, but you have to pay the consequences."

"Not here," he insisted. "A Muslim son is a son for life in Iraq. My brothers, sisters, and I must go to our father for any decisions we make in our life. We have to go to him first."

The significance of his statement impressed me. I saw a side of Iraq I had not seen before, the one that put forth the strong moral fiber of the people in Iraq. Those people were ordinary, good-hearted folks. Our eyes locked as we searched each other's expressions and concentrated intently on what each had to say.

"How do people in America socialize?" he continued.

"What do you mean by socializing?" I replied.

"How often do you see your brothers, your sisters?" he quizzed

"My sister lives about 30 miles away, and I see her sometimes twice a week, but sometimes I will go a month or longer before I see her," Tommy said.

"Not here in Iraq," he said. "I go to my brothers, my sisters, my mother, and my father every week."

That, too, struck me as significant. We talk about family values in America. But we've seemed to lose those kinds of family bonds. Iraq does not have the crime and drug abuse we have in America. They can learn from us, and we can learn from them. There is good in both. We have a lot of things in our country that are headed in the wrong direction.

I wondered, *What are the chances a simple farmer from*

Mississippi, who didn't even finish high school, much less go to college, would be caught up in the middle of all of this. God must have planned this for a long time. Some things I will never understand or know why they happened. I am not sure why those brothers wanted to meet me, but I know meeting them touched my life in a positive way. I suppose they felt that way, too. God truly works in mysterious ways.

I knew at that moment that I would go home. I was going to live. I had been given a message, and if I did not make it home that message would not be delivered. The dialogue I shared with that family changed my whole outlook on the way I viewed the Iraqi people. There are good people over there. We are fighting for a worthy cause. The bad guys are just getting in the way of the freedom and progress of the good people. Islamic extremists and terrorists must be dealt with, and those Americans who want to sit back and do nothing are in denial about the value of the work our troops are doing to help bring democracy to the Iraqi people.

It was late in the afternoon when my captors brought me once again to the L-shaped house. Grasping for the familiar, I looked around the room until I found my lizards to help occupy my mind and help pass the time.

I prepared an injection of antibiotics and gave it to myself in my left hip. After the needle penetrated the skin I slowly injected the antibiotic. It didn't burn like when Moe or Curly injected the medicine too fast.

We immediately returned to our routine, and they brought the "usual" for dinner. I was tired. With all of the activity of the day before I didn't get much sleep, so right after dinner, just after sunset, I laid down with the intention of going to sleep.

But I heard a scratching noise coming from the base of the wall underneath the concrete foundation below the window. Pretty soon a large rat eased out into the room and started toward me. I moved and startled him, and he ran back into his hole. About 10 minutes later he came back into the room. His whiskers twitching as he sniffed the air for the aroma of raw meat. Larry came in to check on me, and I said, "There's an animal, a rat animal, in here!"

He went outside, found part of a hacksaw frame, stuck it down the rat hole, and shoved it in with his foot. He added a concrete block for extra security. Larry went back outside, thinking his job was finished. I lay there with the lantern flickering next to me. The scratching began again. He was a persistent little fellow. He wanted in.

I sat up, leaned against the wall and watched the hole under the concrete block. The dirt began moving. After he tunneled his way to the surface his head popped up, and his beady eyes peered around the room. Thinking the coast was clear, he slinked back into the room. The rat crept along in my direction. He got within a couple of feet and I moved my foot. He darted back into the newly created hole.

I was tired and needed some sleep, but I knew I couldn't sleep with that rat coming in and out of the room. I figured if there was one, there were probably a half-dozen more. I knew that if I let my guard down, I might be eaten alive by a swarm of rats. At the very least, one rat biting me would probably lead to an awful infection that might kill me in my weakened condition.

We played the cat-and-mouse game for another 15 minutes. When he ran back into his hole again, I picked up a brickbat lying in the floor and hovered over to the hole and waited. When he came back out and started down the wall I slung the brick left-handed and missed the rat, bashing the wall instead.

The awful racket brought Larry on the run. He glared at me and I pleaded, "There's a rat! That animal is back!"

Larry motioned that he would go down one wall to corner the rat. I picked up the half brick and started along the other wall. We worked as a team. He and I slowly backed the rat into the corner. Then, the rat broke for cover and scurried under a concrete block. Larry rushed over, grabbed the block, and rocked it back and forth, mashing the rat into the dirt. After squashing the rat, he turned the block over, picked the dead rodent up by the tail and showed it to me proving that the problem was solved. No more rat. No more noisy hostage to disturb his sleep. Thankfully, no more rats tried to get in my cell that night.

I wasn't served any meat the next day, so I felt sure that Larry had disposed of the rat properly.

CHAPTER
14

SUNDAY,
APRIL 18, 2004
IRAQ

TO KILL OR
NOT TO KILL

I woke on the tenth day of my captivity looking for the three lizards. I searched for a while before I spotted one's head poking out of a tiny hole in the wall. Then I spied another in a crack. They then ran down the wall and hung out high above the empty light socket. Watching them occupied my time until Moe and Larry showed up with breakfast.

Before the men arrived I gave myself a shot of antibiotic. I wanted to beat them to the punch. There was no way I was going to let one of them serve as nurse. They didn't know what they were doing. I did a much better job.

"Are you a Christian or Islamic, Muslim?" Moe asked as he made the Catholic sign of the cross.

"I am a Christian," I respond almost before he completed his question.

140

"If you want to be Muslim, we can give you a wife," he said trying a new tactic. "We can give you a store in Baghdad. You can run this store and live here." I figured they probably had the ability to get that done.

"I am a Christian. I have a wife; I've got two children in America. I am going home to see them. One day."

"If I come to America, you give me a wife?" was his retort.

"I can't give you a wife," I said. "That's not the way it works in America. I could introduce you to a woman, but that's as far as I can go."

"I see," he said not really understanding. I think Moe was impressed with me not giving in to him and standing my ground concerning my faith. They were not going to break me down or change me, and they were finally starting to understand. If I had said just once that I was not a Christian and wanted to convert to Islam, the entire situation might have changed.

Suddenly, Moe noticed a wet spot on the dirt floor, where, during the night, I fumbled a bottle of water, and it soaked a small part of the floor before I could clean it up. "Don't do that," he said pointing to the wet spot, thinking I had urinated on the floor. "Go outside." I tried to explain what happened, but he had his mind made up; I had urinated on the floor and that was that.

"It is just water. I spilled water," I said.

"Do not do that in here, go outside," he demanded.

"Okay," I said conceding the argument.

With our conversation over, we sat down to breakfast. It was the usual fare: clabbered milk, leaven bread, water, and *shaay*. Moe was in a mood for chatting and decided to hang around and talk a while. He leaned his AK-47 against the wall next to the door.

"Smoke?" Moe asked as he popped the pack of Iraqi-made cigarettes against his finger.

"No, bad for your health," I stated as he lit up.

"Did you like the food?" he quizzed.

"Yes, the food was good. I am full. Aren't you a farmer?" I asked.

"Yes, I farm and my family does, too," Moe said.

"I milk cows," I replied as I made a downward milking motion with my hands. "I am a farmer, too, a dairy farmer."

"I am a college student in Baghdad," Moe revealed. "I have not been able to go to school this week because I am here guarding you. College is free. That is the only way I can go."

"That is good," I said. "I wish it were free in the United States."

"Yes, it is good. My professor does not make much money though," Moe said.

"What do you think about Saddam?" I asked.

"I am glad he is gone," Moe said. "I do not like Saddam. Before, when Saddam was president, if you lived in Baghdad or in Tikrit, you didn't have much, but you had basic necessities. Food was available, and you had fresh drinking water. If you lived in the country, like I do here, you had to grow your own food. Our drinking water came from the irrigation ditches or wherever we could find it. Now we get bottled water. But I don't want Americans here."

With that last statement the conversation ended. He got up and walked toward the door. As he stepped through the opening, I was shocked to see his rifle still leaning next to the door. All four men were standing together outside with no weapon. They had only the one gun between them. My mind raced. Thoughts flashed through my mind in milliseconds. I had to make a decision in a heartbeat. *I can grab the gun, figure out where the safety is, walk outside, and kill all of these men,* my mind raced. *I can jump in their car and drive to safety.*

Seconds ticked by. Instinct told me to grab the gun and start firing. But, that's not what God wanted me to do. I relaxed and decided not to make that move. I am confident I could have pulled it off, but I went to Iraq to work, to make a better life for my family in Mississippi, not to take a life. I did not go with a weapon in my hand. I didn't go as a soldier. Realizing he had left his gun behind, Moe opened the door just wide enough to reach in, grab the gun by the barrel, and step back out without looking at me or saying a word.

I could not shoot those men. They, I believed, were the angels I asked for. God sent them to me, and they treated me very well. They did not mistreat me in any way. I told myself, *I'm not going to go out there and shoot these men, because I may end up with another group tomorrow that will kill me.*

That could have been my only chance, but that is where my faith took over. I had faith and trust that God was going to get me out of that place and send me home to my family.

Moe and Larry did not come in to pray that morning as they had the two previous days, but they returned at noon with our lunch. The food was good; it was similar to what I eat at home. Although we did not have meat with any meal, the cucumbers, tomatoes, okra, and rice was just good ole country cooking.

Moe and Larry did come in for afternoon prayer around midafternoon. They alternated as usual, staying only a couple of minutes each.

I gave myself the evening antibiotic injection, then prayed:

God, it is all in your hands. You pick the time and place. I will know when that time is. You open the door, and I will be there.

Moe, Larry, Curly, and The Quiet One slept in the room with me that night for the first time. Nothing was ever said about the abandoned gun by any of us. I wondered if Moe had a clue what he had done or what ran through my mind? If he did, it did not show. Was it a test given by my guards, or was it a greater test of faith overseen by God?

I went to sleep that night knowing I had made the right decision.

Tommy adjusts a milking machine at home in Mississippi.
Moe, one of Tommy's guards, seemed to understand
that he was a dairy farmer.

CHAPTER 15

FOLLOW-UP OPERATION

Rousing from sleep's fog, I scanned the room and met eyes with Curly. Acknowledging our eye contact, he started the morning's conversation by flaring his nostrils and snorting at me like a hog. I didn't have long to wonder if Curly had gone crazy when he pointed at me and said, "You snore. You snore loud." At least The Three Stooges and The Quiet One didn't snore and wake me up.

Curly changed the subject, put on an ear-to-ear grin, raised his hands high above his head and, piercingly announced, "Mister, Mister. America. You go to America. Two days go to America!" while he mimicked an airplane rising into flight.

"Good, good," I said, showing no emotion to his declaration, other than a half-smile. I did not ask any questions or get excited as the eleventh day of my captivity began.

Moe walked toward me and outstretched his arm and curled his fingers into a gesture that resembled a rake. With a pulling motion he mocked scratching in the dirt. "Farmer. Plow, yes?" he asked. "We have seen your tractors on TV."

"Yeah, plow," I responded. "Yes, I'm a farmer. I am a dairy farmer. I milk cows."

"Red tractors," Moe added.

"Yes, I have red International tractors."

They had seen my farm on television, and that helped my situation and credibility. I had been telling them I was a farmer, and the clip they had seen on TV validated what I had been telling them all along. It proved I was not lying and could be trusted.

We did not have breakfast that morning; instead they led me to the car once again. We proceeded back to the doctor's house. Both surgeons were present. During our earlier encounter when they performed the first surgery, they had told me that more surgery was required. I knew what to expect.

I sat down. They laid their instruments out and began cleaning them with iodine. The oozing wound had saturated the bandages, which remained stuck to my arm. They used a saline solution to soak the dressing so it could be removed. Even so, the gauze pulled at my skin as they unwrapped it. Though the wound looked like real red hamburger meat, I experienced no significant pain.

From the start of my ordeal I had asked God to take away the pain as much as he could. I prayed:

God, I'll endure as much as you leave for me. If you can ease some of the pain, I will take the rest.

My arm never hurt anymore than a mild headache. It throbbed some, which I viewed as good; that meant blood was pumping through the injured area.

I had been watching the son of The Quiet One, a young boy who looked to be 11 or 12 years of age, standing behind one of the doctors. Our eyes locked, and suddenly tears burst forth and streamed down his young face. He was crying because of what he was seeing. He had feelings and compassion for me. Nearly a teenager, he was almost as old as some of my gun-toting captors, yet he showed heart for a stranger, an American, a man whom many of his countrymen hated. I smiled at him as the doctors repositioned my arm.

One surgeon used a pair of clamps to grab and pull up the dead skin and tissue while the other doctor cut it away. I decided to talk with the surgeon who had talked with me the first time they cut on my arm, the doctor who wanted to know why America was in Iraq. As he worked, I reminded him, "A few days ago, you asked why we are in your country. We are here because of 9/11. I don't know if Saddam was directly or indirectly involved, but we feel he was associated with the people who had something to do with 9/11. There were 3,000 people killed, civilian people. If they would have come over and attacked our military, that would have been bad enough, but to come to our country and attack innocent civilians was despicable."

"We had the same thing happen during our sanctions that started in the early '90s," he replied. "We had thousands of children die here. We had an epidemic; we couldn't get the serum, the medication, we needed to treat them."

I felt compassion for their children, but it didn't make me feel any better about what happened on 9/11. They could have had all the medicine they needed if their dictator hadn't diverted his country's oil-for-food profits as a political weapon and to build new palaces.

When they started cutting, they lifted up a small flap of muscle to expose and remove the dead tissue from beneath it. After they trimmed off the rotting tissue, they laid the flap of living muscle, about the size of a tennis ball, back down. The doctor said it would grow back. The wound site bled a lot after they finished, but he said that was a good sign. Satisfied with their work, they assured me that it would heal in time.

We ate breakfast at the doctor's house. I thanked the doctors as we left. I never saw them again. We headed back to the L-shaped building where we had our typical lunch and dinner.

Later that night they brought in three men whom I had not seen before. One man was dressed very nicely. He wore dark pleated pants that were crisp and shiny, a pressed, light gray cotton shirt, and polished black penny loafers. His face was completely wrapped in a purple headdress. His clothes didn't look like he had worn them for four or five days like mine did. He looked important. One of the other men had his face wrapped in a red headdress. The third man was a short, heavy-set young man carrying a small hand-held video camera. He walked into the room with the camera rolling, taping me as I remained on the floor. He never asked me to speak or do anything.

The door to the building was open, and I could see the car they were driving looked like the vehicle of a dignitary. It was a big, expensive-looking car with curtains surrounding the backseat windows.

"What do you do?" asked the well-dressed man.

"I am a civilian contractor," I replied.

"You are a soldier," pronounced the well-dressed man. "You haul supplies and fuel to soldiers for the trucks, tanks, and planes that bomb Fallujah."

"You are a soldier!" said the man in the red wrap.

"No, I am not a soldier," I said. "I am here to support the military. I am a truck driver."

"You were driving military trucks, no?" said the well-dressed man.

"Yes, I was, but I am a civilian," I said.

"You are a soldier," he said.

The manner in which they treated a soldier would be the way I would be treated. They considered me a soldier no matter what I said.

"Get up," he demanded and then walked me out the door to the car.

He opened the car door and demanded, "We want you to listen to the radio. That's BBC. Now listen."

That seemed odd, but I crawled into the backseat and lay down. The radio was playing and tuned to the BBC

Radio Network. They all went back inside leaving me alone to listen. I was not familiar with BBC radio. I thought it was an all-news station, but they played a documentary about some man of historical importance. I listened to what this guy did back in the 1700s, but I was really hoping to hear some current news. When the news did come on, they ran only a short piece about a Danish man who had been taken hostage south of Baghdad and three journalists who were taken near Najaf, I believe.

I was puzzled. I did not understand the purpose of listening to the BBC. Maybe they thought there would be some news about me. They came out to the car periodically and asked, "Have you heard?"

I would say, "No, I haven't heard anything," not really knowing what it was I was supposed to be hearing in the first place.

The BBC ran another documentary, and the same news about the Danish man and the three journalists ran two or three times more. I stayed out there for at least an hour, and then they took me back into the building. The two strangers got in their car and left. The man with the video camera stayed behind.

I concluded that they had held a meeting of some sort inside while confining me to the car and making me listen to the BBC. They may have been discussing my fate or trying to determine if I was really in the military. Whatever the purpose, it was peculiar.

After about 15 to 20 minutes, they returned, but they did not come inside. They talked with the guy who carried the video camera, then left again. Shortly, Moe, Larry, and Curley showed up along with the doctor, who blindfolded me again. They put me in the doctor's car and drove for more than an hour. We pulled up in front of a tiny shack. It was too dark to tell much about the exterior or where we were. We walked around to the backside of the shack; I followed the doctor and a teenage boy, who led the way with a lantern. There were other teenagers there, but I couldn't see all of them. We entered the shack by squeezing through a small opening that was perhaps two feet square.

Moe, Larry, and Curly fed the sleeping pads, supplies to clean my wound, medicine, and syringes through the small opening. A few minutes later, I heard them climb into the car and drive away. Some of the teenagers remained outside to act as guards.

The doctor and the one teenage boy slept in the shack with me that night. The doctor spoke only a little broken English; so, we did not talk at all.

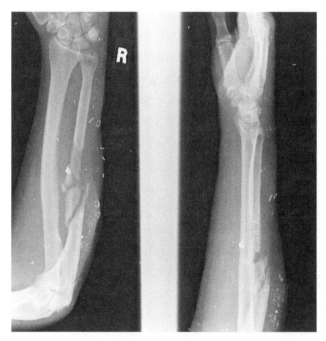

X-rays of Tommy's right arm reveal the damage done during the attack on his convoy.

CHAPTER
16

TUESDAY,
APRIL 20, 2004
IRAQ

THE TOOL SHED

I woke the morning of my twelfth day of captivity and asked if I could go to the bathroom. They let me go outside without a blindfold. We were way out in the desert, a vast expanse of open land with no houses or structures in sight. The homesite had not been occupied for many years. The walls of the outhouse, which lacked a roof, consisted of only two or three courses of masonry block. Inside I found nothing more than a hole in the ground. I took care of business and went back inside.

There was not much to eat for breakfast, only sliced cucumbers, cookies, and water. They also left behind an orange soda and what they called "Pepsi," but it had a different name. After we ate the meal together they secured the door, I heard a car engine crank and someone sped away.

They left behind a makeshift urinal, which was an old vegetable-oil can about eight inches square and 16 inches tall with its top cut off. I felt like a kitten locked in the bathroom while its owners were out for the day.

Apparently this shack had been prepared for me. It smelled of fresh mortar and reminded me of the way a concrete highway smells after a summer rain. I looked around and noticed the grout was still wet where the main door had been walled up. Obviously, they had knocked a hole in the back wall to create the new entryway. There were no windows, only a narrow transom above the place where the old main door had once been. A tiny slit between the old doorframe and the wall offered my only view of the outside world. Even with that, my view was limited to just a few feet.

That night, four boys, maybe 18 or 19 years old, arrived in a car to pick up the doctor and the teenager who had shared the shed with me the night before. When they left, two of the boys remained, each was armed with an AK-47. Before leaving the room, they placed a stainless steel pan full of boiled chicken on the floor and asked, "You like fish?" I nodded yes. "We bring you fish, bring fish next time."

I said, "Okay."

The boys stayed outside leaving me alone. They went behind the tool shed and started a target practice session, firing numerous rounds.

Coal-black dark is the best way to describe night in the tool shed. They didn't leave a lantern or any other means for lighting the room, and with no windows, the shack was sealed from moonlight. Not much breeze circulated through there either, and the air was as stale as a smoky pool hall. Plus, there was a constant array of scratching sounds from mystery critters that crawled and skittered around in the dark. I just knew a snake, hunting for mice, was crawling around in that room. My memories of snake encounters back home and the stories I had heard of vipers found in Iraq didn't help. It was hard to sleep in that hot box. I slept for only 10 to 15 minutes at a time and thought daylight would never arrive in that place.

Life in the country back in rural Mississippi means that snakes are regular visitors. One evening I pulled into our carport and stepped out of the truck like I had a thousand times before. I slammed the door and immediately heard a loud hissing sound. I figured that I had picked up a nail in a tire and had an impending flat to fix. I listened to try and figure out which tire was losing air, but the hissing turned to a loud buzzing. I realized then that a snake might be curled up somewhere near. In the dim light, I could see a timber rattler, about 5 feet long, coiled up by the back steps. Luckily, the snake didn't strike at me when I walked closer. I went inside and grabbed my .32 pistol and shot it to death. That was a close call but nothing I hadn't experienced before, nor do I expect to avoid other snake encounters in the future.

Most of that long night I stayed awake, sitting with my legs folded and tucked underneath me, leaning against the wall waiting for sunrise. Daylight brought a reprieve from the vagueness of the dark and drove my unwelcome visitors into hiding.

*Responding to insurgent gunfire, American soldiers
conduct a dismounted patrol during night operations.*

CHAPTER
17

**WEDNESDAY,
APRIL 21, 2004
IRAQ**

SNAPPY MAKES
A VIDEO

My thirteenth day of captivity, the boys let me out only long enough to make a quick trip to the dilapidated outhouse. I returned to the shack, ate a few cookies, and drank some water. I continued to give myself an antibiotic shot. Thank goodness the doctor had provided an ample supply of individually wrapped syringes.

Injecting myself proved to be a little uncomfortable, but not as difficult as I would have imagined. Considering my situation and the severe infection in my wounded arm, I had to take the shots, and the injection didn't hurt as bad when I did it. The Three Stooges injected the medicine too fast, which burned. Because of my injured arm I could only inject myself in the left hip; they alternated hips when they gave the injections.

The doctor also left some pills. He instructed me to take one every six hours. I had no idea what they were, but I took them anyway. I felt no ill effects from whatever medication they contained, no drugged feeling.

About midmorning the boys came in with a man I had not met before. He was carrying a video camera, and, like The Three Stooges, wore a white robe. He was heavy-set, sort of barrel-chested, and wore a trimmed but scruffy beard. He was a spitting image of Berroq, the character in *Indiana Jones and the Raiders of the Lost Ark* who was Indy's guide. I came to think of him as "Snappy." In the beginning Snappy was soft spoken and quiet, but that was about to change.

In a low voice, almost a whisper, he said, "We want you to ask for your release. But we want you to ask humanitarian organizations for your release."

He turned on the camera, pointed at me, and I said, "I want to ask the government organi…"

"Stop!" His temper flared with a vengeance. Snappy continued to shout, "I did not say government! I said nothing about government, nothing. They are not humanitarian. You talk about humanitarian organizations. Now go."

"I would like to appeal to any humanitarian organization, from any country that would be willing to negotiate my release."

That was it. He was satisfied and promptly left taking everybody with him. I was left alone for the day, which was fine with me.

I did not mind being left by myself at all. Loneliness is

not an emotion I have experienced only in Iraq. It is a feeling I am very familiar with. When making long-distance runs, while driving a truck from Mississippi to places like New York, Ohio, or California, I would get an urgent feeling that I wanted to be home at that very moment. A feeling of isolation and lonesomeness would set in, but God took those sensations away while I was in captivity.

Being alone has been part of my job description my entire career. As a truck driver, I have driven three million miles — alone. Dairy farming isn't much different. Most of my chores I did without help. It was no big deal now for me to be left alone in the wilderness. Other folks with different backgrounds or careers may have felt lonely, but I did not experience that emotion.

I never felt anxious or fearful, either. I had suffered anxiety attacks at home while trying to cope with running a farm and worrying if there would be enough cash flow to meet the bank note and pay the bills. Small farmers know what stress and anxiety is all about. The emotions I felt in Iraq were nothing compared to the struggles farmers face as they fight to save their ways of life.

I did not concern myself with "passing the time" or "keeping busy." Daylight hours were often the best time to sleep. The creepy crawly animals were hiding and the mosquitoes were not as bad during the day. When I could, I looked outside and surveyed the landscape or watched for human activity.

That night was as dark and restless as the night before. Daylight seemed like it would never come.

Tommy feels at home behind the wheel of a "big rig."

CHAPTER
18

THURSDAY,
APRIL 22, 2004
IRAQ

THE
BREAK-IN

There was still no one else at the shack as morning broke. I wondered if the others would return at all that day. Time had ceased to have much meaning, and as the days ran together, I lost count of how long I had been in captivity. I didn't know what day of the week it was, and I thought it could be Wednesday, Thursday, or Friday. It didn't matter because I had no control over the situation, and I was going to take it one day at a time no matter the day. I prayed:

God, I do not know how long I am going to be here. I realize we have had soldiers in past wars who were in prison camps for years and years. I do not have any idea how long I will be here. You pick a time and a day and a place in the future and I will know that day, I will know that is the day you have picked.

I heard helicopters in the distance off and on. I tried to figure out where in Iraq I was and wanted to see behind the shack. On the back wall there was a small hole that was just barely too high for me to look through. But the men had left all of their pads and pillows from the first night. I had stacked them on top of each other the previous night to create a thicker, softer bed. Then I decided to use them to benefit in another way.

I folded and stacked the bedding under the hole in the back wall. Standing on top of the pile, I was able to see through the hole, which gave me a good view of a canal that flowed just behind the shack. Beyond the waterway about a mile and out of hearing distance, I could see bulldozers pushing up sand. At the farthest point of my vision, smokestacks bellowed plumes of soot. While driving trucks through Iraq, I had seen similar smokestacks and thought I might be close to Baghdad.

I polished the stainless steel pan that held my chicken meal. I polished it to a shine by rubbing it with my hand and my shirtsleeve. I stuck it through the hole and let the sun hit it directly. The pan reflected a brilliant light. If a helicopter happened to fly near, I planned to use the pan to send a signal and hoped someone would want to investigate.

I sat back down and even dozed off for a couple of hours, but the sound of a helicopter woke me. I jumped up and climbed on the mountain of pads for a look. There was a Blackhawk, flying low from east to west, straight at the shack. I needed to have been a little higher, but I stuck the pan through the hole, aimed it at the sun, and twitched it at the copter. As it passed overhead I could see the cross on its side. It was a Medivac helicopter. It sped by without seeing my signal.

I recognized that this was not the time for my rescue. God would choose the time, but I had to do my part. I was not going to just sit there passively and wait to be lifted up out of there. I would have to be diligent and be ready to act when the time came.

Looking around the room for other possible means of escape I noticed the mortar was still damp around the door. I looked up at the rafters and saw a piece of timber sticking out. Stacking the pads and pillows I climbed on top and managed to grab the wood. I didn't have much leverage or pulling power with just one arm but I fought with it until a four-foot section broke off.

I moved the pads back under the high hole in the wall, in case another chopper flew by, and started pushing with the timber at the wet mortar, which fell away in small chunks. I wasn't sure that I was accomplishing anything so I thought it best to wait and see what happened later. I put the timber back up in the rafters, where I could retrieve it later if need be.

Later that afternoon I heard a vehicle come to a stop outside. The door opened, and I could hear an adult and a couple of kids speaking in Arabic. They walked around to the backside of the building to the narrow door and began hollering. I did not say a word. I just remained still.

I don't understand much Arabic, but I think they were saying something like, "Hey, who is in there? Say something." The next thing I knew, a thin piece of a flat bar came through the slit in the door. They were prying and pushing, trying to force the door aside to get in.

I thought to myself, *two things can happen: either they get the door open and I escape, or they won't be able to pry it open. When the bad guys return and see the door has been tampered with, they'll think I've tried to escape, and that's all the excuse they will need to shoot me.*

The man pried it open enough to get his fist through. I could see him looking around inside. He could not see me because I was backed into a dark corner. I decided I would see if they would help me. I walked over to the door and peered out. There stood a man in his thirties with two young boys, one on each side of him. Just behind them was their early-model Datsun pickup. Its white, beat-up body was rusted along the bottom edge and around the wheel wells.

"Can you open the door?" I implored. "Can you pull the latch? If you can't, can you go to the U.S. soldiers or the Iraqi police and bring them back here? Can you take me to them?"

They started backing up and talking really fast in Arabic. I knew they had not understood anything I said. They climbed into the truck, never taking their eye off where I was standing, and drove away. I never saw them again.

They had created a big crack at the edge of the door by bending the metal frame. The hole was large enough for me to run my arm through, but the latch was just out of reach. The door was also secured with an eight-foot-long concrete fence post wedged between the ground and the door. One end of the post was broken off, and the rebar reinforcement jutting from the concrete dug into the outside of the door. As hard as I pushed, I could not budge it.

It was getting late, and I knew that if my captors were to return it would be soon. I decided I needed to repair the damage done to the door by the man and his sons. I pushed the metal back in the way it had been and tried to beat it back to its original shape. It was still messed up; I just hoped they wouldn't notice. If they thought I had almost broken out there could be serious consequences.

As the darkest of nights crawled by, I knew they were not coming back that evening. I thought that would give me another day to work on the door, either to open or repair it.

Sleeping was difficult in that dark little shack. With no light source, I literally could not see my hand when I held it in front of my eyes. I could hear things crawling on the floor and walls. I didn't know whether they were rats, spiders, lizards, or snakes. I knew several types of vipers call that desert home. The horned viper may be the worst. I had been told their venom causes severe internal bleeding and death. Other snakes lived in Iraq that I couldn't identify but were just as deadly. Scorpion bites can cause asphyxiation. Then there is the golf-ball-sized camel spider. Even if they didn't bite you, they could cause a fellow to hurt himself trying to get away.

Many of these dangerous creatures are nocturnal hunters and seek warmth on cool nights. With the nightly desert temperatures falling to the mid-50s, that rundown shack offered the perfect shelter for them. I was more concerned about the creatures of the night than I was about the militants holding me hostage.

While I sat there in the dark I recalled another snake encounter of my youth. I've always had a healthy fear of snakes. As a youth I often followed my father for about a mile through the woods and fields behind our house to the river, where we often caught catfish. Daddy never hesitated to wade through the waist-high weeds, ignoring the copperheads, cottonmouths, and rattlesnakes that lived there in abundance. We'd always fish until late and walk home in the fading light. Struggling to keep up, I picked my way carefully looking for "Mr. No-Shoulders." One time, when my dad walked ahead, I spied a 5-foot-long snake in the path and called my father back to take care of it. He cut a limb and just shooed it out of the way like it was a stray calf.

All I could do was wait until morning to see what was sharing my prison.

FRIDAY,
APRIL 23, 2004
IRAQ

FIRST ESCAPE

Fortunately, when morning came I was the only living thing in the room. There is no doubt I had visitors during the night before my fifteenth day of captivity.

As the sun began to crest the horizon I heard the distant sound of helicopters. Hurriedly I ran over to the door, looked through the slit, and saw the far-off dots of five or more helicopters coming in my direction. I began pulling the metal back from around the doorframe, where the Iraqi man had forced it, and expanded the size of the hole.

I ran my arm through and tried to grab the latch, but it was still beyond my reach. I knew even if I could reach the latch it would be very difficult to unhitch. The day before, my Iraqi visitors had been standing on the outside with the latch within easy reach, but could not open it. But I had to try. Time was short.

I grabbed the timber from the rafters, jammed it into the

crack, and commenced prying as hard as I could. I managed to make the opening bigger, and that enabled me to reach the latch, but it wouldn't budge. The throw bolt was wedged firmly into the receiver.

I put my shoulder to the door and pushed while I manipulated the latch. It worked! The latch opened. I thought I would be able to push my way out, but the concrete fence post would not move.

A piece of rebar protruded from the post and formed a loop. I worked the timber through the loop and pried against the doorframe. I had to use my injured right arm to pull down on the timber that held the post up away from the door. It wouldn't budge. I shifted my body so I could get my left arm through the opening. I pushed at the post until it swung free and dropped away from the door.

I shoved the door open and ran outside but turned around to retrieve the black-and-white blindfold. I found a long stick outside and quickly tied the blindfold on one end. There were two huge mounds of dirt that were the result of a bulldozer digging a deep water hole. The piles were about 30 to 40 feet high.

I ran up the first mound I came to. The helicopters were still a half-mile away but angling in my direction. There was one Chinook and four Blackhawks spread out in an irregular pattern across the sky. I started waving the heavy stick and my right arm. They flew by about a quarter-mile away. They could have easily seen me but might have thought that I was an Iraqi kid waving at them.

They kept going, but I was outside with no guards

around — my first taste of freedom in more than two weeks. I could see several square miles of desert and saw people walking around a factory of some sort about a mile away. I hunted around for a smaller stick that would be easier to wave around than the cumbersome board I had just used. I found a short limb and tied the blindfold to one end.

It felt good to be out walking around with no one watching over me, but I wondered where the helicopters were headed. If they were coming out of the west, then they were leaving a camp near the Syrian border, a camp that was part of our delivery route. Or the choppers might have been headed to BIAP air base. I still did not know where I was. I could have been in a totally different part of Iraq from where I had been captured. All I really knew was that I was in the desert.

I had less than a bottle of water left. It had been two days since I had seen my captors. I reasoned they were probably coming back at dark. I could see for 10 miles in all directions. Which way should I go? But if I started walking, my water wouldn't last long enough. If I had to ask somebody for water and they caught me, they would most assuredly kill me. I ruled out trying to hike my way to freedom.

From the big mound of dirt, I could see that the factory was active. Dump trucks were hauling some material out of the area. A couple of men walked around outside the building. I thought if they left a truck unattended, I could hot-wire it and drive out that night. But later that day the drivers got in the trucks and drove away. There was one pickup truck still parked outside the building. I waited, thinking it may offer an opportunity, but before long a man came out, got in, and drove off. I had to think of another way.

The other mound had a steep side that I thought would make a perfect drawing board for a rescue signal. I took my sandal and raked out the letters H and E. I backed off to check my work but could not see the letters very well, plus I was wearing myself out digging a message into the side of that hill. So, I took off my black shirt, tied it to the limb, then tied the blindfold onto the end of the shirt and sat there and waited.

Several hours passed before I heard helicopters approaching from the west. There were two big twin-rotor Chinook transports making a beeline toward me. There was no way they couldn't see me. I started waving the limb and my right arm with its white bandage. There I was, a white man in the middle of Iraq, waving a flag on top of a huge mound of dirt. How could I make myself more visible?

I smiled, for the first time in days, as they got closer. I thought to myself, *This is it. I am going to be out of here today.* I envisioned the helicopters slowing down, hovering, and coming in for a landing. I could see the pilot sitting at the controls of one of the choppers. They flew over. I turned and could see a soldier in the back. I thought they had surely seen me. They made a bobble back and forth and away they went. They didn't check up.

I thought that maybe they saw me and would radio for

someone else to come get me. Maybe there would be a Humvee close or a patrol that they could call. That didn't happen.

My options had expired for the day. I had no other choice but to get back in the shack and lock myself in. I went back inside, locked the latch, pulled the concrete post back against the door, and sat down.

As night fell I thought my captors would be back soon. It wasn't long before I heard a car barreling down the road.

They usually walked up to the door, moved the post over, unlatched the door, and walked in. This time they stopped in front of the door and talked for a couple of minutes. I had tried covering my tracks and securing the door back as it was, but I just knew I had been caught.

They pulled the door open, came in, and put a tray down. Sure enough they had brought fish, a huge baked fish that they had partly eaten. Snappy walked over to me and said, "Did you do that?" as he pointed to the door.

"Naw, an Iraqi man and his two sons came by. They were curious and pried it open."

I never told them I got out.

They watched me eat the fish. I told them I had enough, and they all left. They did not even leave a guard. I figured I would not see them again for two more days.

I settled in for the night, along with all the noisy crawly things. Then somewhere around midnight I heard a car pull up and stop. They had returned. Snappy came in and ordered me to get up. The teenage boys grabbed all of my medical supplies, pads, blankets, and pillows and loaded them into the car. We all got into the vehicle. The teenage boys sat on either side of me in the backseat. One of the other teenagers got behind the wheel, and Snappy took the passenger seat.

They did not blindfold me that time. I didn't know where we were going, and they didn't tell me. We traveled along a canal. It was one of Saddam's man-made irrigation canals. They did not seem to know where they were going. We came to a fork in the road, and they argued a few minutes before turning right.

The paved road gave way to a crooked, rough gravel road as we continued the 90-minute journey. At one point during the trip we pulled up to what looked like a store. I could see a man sitting inside behind a counter. I noticed a small dark red car parked on the side of the road.

Snappy and the driver got out and approached the car. Two men got out and they all started talking. They conversed for at least 30 minutes before the occupants of the red car got back in their car. Then the two teens sitting with me got out to have a discussion with Snappy and the driver, leaving me alone in the car. Something was up. I didn't think they knew what to do with me at that point.

The meeting concluded five minutes later, and everybody got back in the car except one of the teens who jumped in the red car. We followed the red car a short distance and made a right turn onto a narrow, one-lane, blacktop road that soon paralleled a gigantic power line. We rode under it for a mile or two and made a right-hand turn onto a dirt road that we traveled for another half-mile.

We pulled up, stopped, and there we were right back at the L-shaped building. It was still dark, probably around three or four in the morning. They escorted me inside and brought along all of my possessions. Everybody left. I was exhausted. We had been on the run since midnight. I stretched out and slept for a couple of hours.

Two CH-47 Chinook helicopters head north in Iraq.

**CHAPTER
20**

SATURDAY,
APRIL 24, 2004
IRAQ

SHACKLES AND
CHAINS

Moe, Larry, and Curly bounced into my cell and acted surprised to see me.

"What are you doing here? Why, why?" asked Moe.

"I don't know," I replied, but thought, *You tell me, you moron. I'm the hostage!*

They left but soon returned with the breakfast I had become accustomed to eating.

"Mister, mister, how are you today mister?" Curly asked, returning to his usual form.

"Okay," I deadpanned.

"We heard Jesse Jackson wants to come negotiate for your release."

I took that to mean that they were going to exchange

me for someone else, but I knew the United States government was not going to do that. I did not want or expect my country to negotiate my release or give in to the demands of hostage takers.

"Going to America, two days," he said as he sat on the floor mocking a pilot sitting in a cockpit during takeoff. "Going to America."

"Whatever." I had heard enough of that.

Moe snatched the black-and-white blindfold, placed it over my eyes, and tied it in a double knot. I had the makings of a beard since I hadn't shaved in more than two weeks, so Moe observed, "Muslim, Muslim, you look like Muslim."

"If you say so."

Curly kept saying, "Two days, go to America." Of course, the two days would come and nothing would happen, but maybe that tied into the Jesse Jackson negotiations.

They escorted me back to the car and put me in the backseat. We rode the short distance back to The Country Place where I had heard the crane and the frogs.

I wasn't there long before Snappy drove up in a light gray car. Then another car pulled up with two men I had not seen before. With three vehicles parked out front, the place started looking like a used car lot. I could feel a hand grasp my arm and we rushed out. I had no idea what direction we were headed, but we rode for about 30 minutes. The man sitting next to me unexpectedly removed my blindfold and asked, "Do you recognize me? Do you know who I am?"

How Snappy could think I would not recognize him

was beyond understanding. I said, "Sure. You were with me at the shed in the desert and did the video."

We were following the four men in the same red car as the night before and driving along a shallow man-made canal. The water was dirty red like it had been stirred up. The red car in front slowed down and turned onto a simple bridge, which was barely wide enough to accommodate one vehicle. The bridge sagged and swayed under the car's weight, but he made it to the other side. We followed.

Once on the other side, we drove inside the levees on crude roads that had been created when the canal was excavated. From above the levees, the cars were hidden from view, and down on the road, we could see only the sky beyond the levee walls. On occasion, we passed little shops along the road. Rather abruptly, Snappy said, "Jesse Jackson is trying to negotiate your release. We get you close to exchange point."

I knew Jesse Jackson had been instrumental in winning the freedom of other hostages during the Gulf War and in Kosovo. I was glad to hear he was involved.

We drove two miles then turned left over a levee to where I could see nothing but hot desert.

We drove for 30 minutes or so. I saw buildings in the distance that looked familiar, but we were on the opposite side from where I had seen them before. We came to a highway and made a left. I thought to myself, *We are about to come to a road that I know.* We took a right and I concluded, *I know where I am.* We were near the northern boundary of our convoy route that ran between Samarra and Fallujah. Had I been aware of that two days ago, I would have left that shack and walked out. The canal we drove along was the same canal that I saw through the hole in the wall.

I could have walked down to that canal, turned either east or west, and made it to safety. In one direction, I could have hiked right to that road. KBR convoys used that highway every day. I could have easily flagged down a truck. Or, in the other direction, there was a camp another 8 to 10 miles away. I could have walked that far without any water. My mind raced, if only I had known.

I grimaced at the missed opportunity, but at least I gained some bearings. If they put me in another house either in the same area, near the canals, or back in the shack, I knew what to do if I ever got out again. I felt like I could have escaped from most of the buildings they used as holding cells. In the L-shaped building, I could have knocked out the angle iron and squeezed through the opening. If only the right opportunity would come along.

I was still relying on God to provide a means for my escape. I was still at peace with my situation. I was not anxious or nervous and felt no sense of urgency.

We continued on the highway beside a river that flowed from north to south, headed toward the town of Samarra. I had made runs from Camp Anaconda driving through Samarra before turning onto the highway that ran next to the river toward Fallujah. The last time I made that run there was a checkpoint south of Samarra.

We kept following the red car. Both cars stopped when

they saw the checkpoint. After a brief pause, the red car went toward the checkpoint while we stayed behind. They returned about 30 minutes later, and they conferred with the guys in the car with me. We eased up the road and crossed a bridge. We pulled onto Highway 1 and drove south. We exited into the parking lot of a restaurant and sat while the men in the red car went ahead to scout for routes around checkpoints.

Snappy went inside the restaurant and came out with a big bag of mixed nuts. He poured me a huge handful of nuts, salty nuts with nothing to drink. I chewed slowly and swallowed them. Snappy stayed outside, leaned against the car, and chomped on his mixed nuts.

I watched for KBR convoys but saw only a lot of local traffic. The little red car returned 20 minutes later. They must have told the folks in my car that we could not get through because we turned around and practically retraced our path. We didn't cross the bridge this time; instead, we turned on the east side of the canal. There was no road, but that did not stop us, we made our own, and eventually wound our way around the first checkpoint. Still, I knew there were two more ahead, and they were major ones. I didn't say anything; I was not about to give them any warning.

The red car was still running interference ahead of our car at a high rate of speed. Suddenly, their car jerked off the road with its emergency flashers going. We stopped behind them, and the two groups huddled again to debate which way to travel. Then we turned around and headed back north. We didn't go far when we turned around again and pulled off the road.

The red car took off on another scouting mission. They returned 15 minutes later with a plan. We headed south again but soon drove off the west side of the road. We bounced through cabbage patches and brush for 30 to 40 minutes picking our way around the checkpoint.

They looked relieved, but I knew there was yet another checkpoint ahead. We got back on the highway and headed south just ahead of a full U.S. Military convoy. I could see the checkpoint tower just in front of us, but they kept heading straight toward it. We ran just shy of the checkpoint and turned into a house only 50 yards off the road. They jumped out, opened the hood, and pretended to be pouring water into the radiator. Snappy swiftly reached over, locked the door, pointed to the convoy, and ordered me to look at him.

If he had not locked that door I might have tried to make a run for the convoy. I don't believe they would have shot me; we were too close to U.S. Military personnel. Our guys would have wiped them out.

Even though I may have missed an opportunity to escape, again, I did not get upset. I still was determined to take each day carefully and flow with the tide.

As soon as the convoy had passed, we turned around, and struck out through the desert. There were small huts everywhere. We stopped at two of them and asked for directions to get around the checkpoint. Something worked because we managed to evade a third checkpoint.

We were on the road again, heading south straight toward Baghdad. Camp Anaconda was just down the road, north of the capital city. We weren't far at all from my camp.

We drove through a small market area with a couple of restaurants and some produce stands. My camp was only 10 more miles south. However, we came to an overpass and took that exit and continued eastbound on a paved road. I had never been to that area of Iraq before.

Tall palm trees and greenery grew all around. Brushy trees, bushes, and low-growing trees replaced the desert sand we had been bouncing over all day. I remembered that the Garden of Eden was supposed to have flourished somewhere in Iraq, and this place was very lush.

We drove through a small town, and one of the teenagers in the car with me started blowing the horn and waving out the window to the bystanders. Apparently, he wanted them to see he was driving an American around. It was like he was saying, "Look at me, I am important. Look who I have in the backseat." Snappy was constantly yelling, "Quit doing that!"

We crossed a canal, made a right turn, and standing in the middle of the road was an Iraqi cop dressed in a uniform of dark blue pants and a light blue shirt. We had no choice; we had to go through that checkpoint. Snappy quickly told me to look the other way. I turned my head and looked out the right window. The cop did not say a word; he just motioned for us to proceed.

Soon we came to the Tigris River, and we crossed over on a floating pontoon bridge that Snappy called the "Saddam

Bridge." Before long, we pulled in behind a stable area and drove up to a house nestled in some small trees.

As we went through the gate Snappy barked at me, "Do not speak, do not look at these people."

"Okay," I simply uttered.

There were a total of eight of us traveling in the two cars. We all walked to the front door where everybody took off their sandals, and I did the same. As we walked in I noticed right away that the house had air conditioning. Two young boys brought pitchers of water to the group. After everybody drank a glass of water they gave me a glassful. On Snappy's orders, one of the men who was with us brought my belongings and set them in a corner of the room.

A man whom I had not seen, wearing a nice, clean, and pressed dark brown robe, came in, and all of the men gave him a hug and a kiss on the cheek. He seemed important, but he did not stay.

They brought in a rug and several small mats. Snappy knelt down on the rug, and the other seven men knelt on the mats. They all began praying aloud in Arabic as I sat and watched.

They were picking up their mats when a short man walked into the room. Immediately they all walked over to him and started their cheek-hug greeting. That was the first time I had witnessed any of my captors making such formal greetings. I assumed he must be somebody important. He did not speak to me, look at me, or acknowledge my presence in any other way. In fact, no one in the room had said a word to me, and I didn't say anything to them.

They eventually put me in another room. Like every other room I had been in so far, there were pads laying on the floor all around the wall's edge. I went to the far corner and laid down facing the wall. People kept entering and leaving the room, but other folks simply walked through.

I dozed off for about 30 minutes. When I woke I could not hear any activity. I didn't know if the people who brought me had left or if the individuals whom I was not supposed to look at were still around. I laid still a few moments then slowly rolled over with my eyes half shut. Peeking through my eyelashes, I could see one guy sitting and another standing. Both wore gray *dishdasha* robes and only their eyes showed through their full head and face wraps. Even with their faces covered I judged them to be 18 to 20 years old. I opened my eyes a little more. The guy sitting had a semi-automatic 9mm pistol in his hand. When he saw me looking at him he raised the gun and pointed it right at my head. The guy standing began talking to him in Arabic.

I turned my back to him and faced the wall again. I stared at the wall for a couple of minutes then decided to give him another try. I rolled back over and looked again. He got up out of his chair and walked toward me. The other man walked with him, talking to him all the way. When he was three feet away he aimed the gun at my head and held it there for about a minute.

The guy doing all the talking told me to sit up. Then he left the room and returned with a small blindfold that was pressed and folded. This blindfold was unlike the others I had been wearing; it was a tan color with some sort of symbols on it and looked like a blindfold suited for someone doomed to be executed. They tied it tight around my eyes. I thought that they might be the ones assigned to kill me.

They grabbed my hands and pulled them up. They slipped something over my wrists, some sort of shackles. The left handcuff fit fine, but my right arm was swollen at the wrist and the device was not large enough to close around it. They squeezed forcefully on the horseshoe-shaped handcuff, which operated on a hinge and was held shut by a screw. They finally closed the cuff around my right wrist and tightened the screw, but not without cutting off the circulation to my hand. The two cuffs were welded together so that my hands were in a crossed position.

One man took hold of my left arm and the other grabbed my injured right arm. Up to that point all of my other captors had avoided even touching my wounded arm. These characters didn't care where on my arm they grabbed. They led me out the door. I didn't know if they had picked up my medical supplies, and I didn't ask.

They shoved me into the front seat of a vehicle. My blindfold was so tight I couldn't even open my eyelids but I knew that the vehicle was a two-seater. I thought it was probably a small pickup truck. They sat me in the middle between the bucket seats next to the standard gear shifter. The driver got irritated because my knees kept getting in the way while he shifted gears.

I could feel the pontoon bridge bobbing and swaying as

we crossed the Tigris River. On the other side, we drove slowly, and I could hear heavy traffic and people talking. I knew we were in some sort of town or city.

Once we passed through the town, we picked up speed. The car was rocking back and forth. I had trouble keeping my balance because of the winding road and the way my hands were shackled. We went into a curve and I fell against the driver. He snapped, "I do not move, I do not move!" I said nothing. I scrunched down a little bit and managed to wedge my knees into the dash and pushed back to maintain my balance.

We drove on for another 20 to 30 minutes, and then stopped abruptly. The two men got out, slammed the doors, and began talking in disagreeable tones. The car doors opened back up, and two other guys jumped in and took over as my newest captors. They spoke softer than the previous two.

We sped down the road for 20 minutes or so. We stopped and they ordered me out of the car. They rushed me to another, bigger vehicle. We roared back onto the road in no time. The windows were rolled down, which helped mitigate the heat. We drove for what seemed like an eternity.

The discomfort of the shackles had grown nearly unbearable, and the fingers on my right hand had gone numb. All of the rocking back and forth did not help and actually made the shackles hurt even more. Finally, I had to speak. I would not have asked or said anything to that first bunch, but I felt that these men were reasonable. "The shackles are hurting," I said.

"Are you okay?" asked one of the new captors.

"Can you take them off?" I asked.

"One o'clock," one of them answered.

I did not know what that meant because it was nowhere near one o'clock, either a.m. or p.m. It was the middle of the afternoon, around three. There was nothing more I felt I could do. I would just wait until "one o'clock."

We continued to ride as the hot winds swirled inside the car. I started to hear frogs croaking along the road. For miles, there were millions of them singing their songs. I smelled the fresh scent of grass and knew there was some kind of water source nearby.

Again I begged, "Can you take off the shackles? They are hurting."

"One o'clock. One o'clock," was his standard answer.

We kept rolling for another 15 to 20 minutes, then stopped and got out. The shackles were killing me. As they dragged me out of the car I asked yet again, "These shackles are hurting, can you please take them off?"

"One o'clock."

He walked me to the front of the car and immediately started removing the shackles. I will never know what "one o'clock" meant. I am not sure he did either.

I felt blessed to have been able to pick up on the manners and behavior of all the captors who had guarded me. Just a little bit of good judgment enabled me to know whom I could talk to, look at, or stand up to while expressing my beliefs. It also enabled me to know when to ask for a little mercy and the smarts to avoid acting disrespectfully, which could have gotten me killed.

Leading me by my left arm, the two men walked me through some trees. They did not touch my wounded right arm. Still blindfolded, I thought to myself, *These guys are going to be all right.*

They sat me down in a patch of soft, fragrant grass. The frogs were croaking at full volume. Within a few more steps, I knew we were close to a river or creek, because I heard the unmistakable sound of water gurgling its way through vegetation. I could smell the fishy scent of the water, and the aroma reminded me of a farm pond back home that was loaded with fish.

I simply sat there waiting on the next move. I heard someone walking through the bushes. He made his way to me and instructed me to get up. I didn't recognize the man's voice, apparently he was yet another guard. He had a very soft, wimpy kind of voice, so I soon thought of him as "Wimpy."

Another man grabbed my left arm and walked me inside a house. He removed my blindfold. There were three men in the room, and they seemed nice enough. I had been thinking about a bath for a while, and I needed one in the worst way. I wanted some water, too, but I did not say a word.

Then a soft-spoken guy wearing a white robe asked from the doorway of another room, "Do you need water?"

"Yes," I said, comforted by the thought of a cool glass of water.

He turned and disappeared. He returned and motioned for me to follow. I went in and noticed a showerhead protruding from the wall — the first indoor shower I had seen since I left Camp Anaconda.

"Do you want me to take a shower?" I asked optimistically.

"Yes," answered the man. I later nicknamed him "The Nice Guy." A shower sounded wonderful, and I am sure they were looking forward to a clean hostage.

The levers didn't work right. I was having a tough time getting any water to flow at all. The Nice Guy came in and adjusted the cold-and-hot-water controls. Perfect. He left the room and I took a long therapeutic shower.

I put the same clothes back on and went back into the room with the other men. I took a seat on one of the everpresent pads. They had brought in my medicine bag containing the syringes, antibiotics, gauze, hydrogen peroxide, and pills. My iodine had been left at the last house, so I was concerned that I didn't have the proper medication to clean my wound. Medical care was left to me, but a thorough cleaning of the wound site with the peroxide and a rewrap with gauze was about all I could do.

Around 9 or 10 that night, The Nice Guy asked if I was ready to eat. I nodded and said "yes." Another soft-spoken man, wearing a dark brown robe, presented a big plate of rice, tomatoes, sliced cucumbers, and a bowl of okra soup. I was hungry; it had been a long time since I had eaten with Moe, Larry, and Curly that morning. They left me alone to eat, and I devoured everything on the plate.

The Nice Guy came in with a pot of *shaay* after I finished the meal. The Nice Guy, another man, and I drank two or three glasses apiece.

After my meal, I prepared to give myself an antibiotic injection. I got the bag, opened it, took out the ingredients, shook up the dosage, and proceeded to give myself the shot. The Nice Guy was watching every step, then he asked, "Are you going to do it yourself?"

"Yes, I am."

He looked amazed that I was giving myself a shot. I gave myself the injection in my left hip again. I did not know if administering a shot in the same hip twice a day was going to cause any problems, but I had no choice.

The Nice Guy and I sat and talked about my condition for a while. He just came across as a good person, one who really didn't want me to be captured. I felt like he wanted me turned loose.

"I am going to have to move you down the street," he said.

"Okay," I said, feeling good about the folks whom I was with at the moment.

We walked to the end of a road to a small storage-type building. Inside, there was an old hand-operated washing machine like we had when I was a kid. There was a basket where the soap and water went and a hand-crank wringer on the top with the two rubberized spools. A couple of old wooden chairs and a handmade wooden bench sat in one corner. The furnishings appeared to have taken punishment from two or three generations of kids.

The three men who lived in the house all came with me

and stayed the night with me. My full belly and a lack of biting insects made it possible for me to get the most restful night's sleep I had while in captivity.

Shackles similar to those used by Tommy's captors.

CHAPTER
21

SUNDAY,
APRIL 25, 2004
IRAQ

LETTER TO
KELLIE

A voice roused me from my deep slumber.

"We are going to get breakfast," The Nice Guy called out.

I rose up on my left elbow and looked around the room. The architecture of my cell wasn't much different from many of the other places they had kept me hidden: crude masonry walls and dirt floors hard as concrete.

The Nice Guy brought back a breakfast that had become very familiar: clabbered milk and leaven bread. For a country boy from Mississippi that fare was quite a leap from grits, biscuits and gravy, sausage, and two eggs over easy, but it seemed to hit the spot each morning. "We are moving you around because of the patrol." As I continued chewing he added, "They are checking houses, so we must keep moving you."

"Yeah, I figured that's why we were moving around so much."

"I hope they turn you loose," he said.

"I hope they let me go home," I replied.

I stayed there most of the seventeenth day of my captivity. The men left for a short while, then returned with two men I didn't recognize. Both men were about 5 feet, 10 inches tall. One spoke English and wore a light tan colored robe. The other man did not speak English and wore a brown robe.

The man who spoke English said of his partner, "He wants to know what you know about the military operations."

"I don't know anything. I am a civilian contractor."

Apparently that was all he wanted from me. They continued talking for a few more minutes, then the man asking the questions left. Maybe my answers satisfied his curiosity.

"Would you like to write a letter to your wife?" The man who spoke English surprisingly quizzed.

"If I do, can you get it to my wife?"

"We can use international telegram."

"Do you have my address?" There was no doubt they already had it, so it was not going to hurt to give it to them again.

"We have your address."

"Do you have my wallet?"

"No, but we can get it back for you."

"All my stuff?"

"We can get it all."

Things are different in Iraq. In the United States once your property is stolen, it's gone and you will probably never see it again. In Iraq, all you have to do is ask for your stuff back, and whoever has it gives it back. They keep nothing. I believed them.

He gave me a sheet of notebook paper and a black ink pen and I wrote to Kellie: "How are you doing? I have been thinking about you and the kids. I want you to know I am fine. These people have been taking good care of me. I have made it this far and they have not harmed me. I feel sure I will be coming home. I don't know when, but I believe it will happen. Just wait, I will be there one day."

I folded it up and handed it back to him. He said, "Islam has said you will not be killed." Up to that point, none of my captors had given me any clue what they had planned for me. No doubt, I took it as good news, but I did not change my expression. I thought to myself, *I hope they keep me with this guy. He has a lot of compassion for me. He wants me released. Maybe he will be the one who turns me loose.*

Then, I wondered if they did release me how it would take place? *I know they can't take me out somewhere and just leave me. Somebody would pick me up and they won't be as nice as these guys. Maybe they'll contact al-Jazeera and tell them they are releasing a hostage.*

That night The Nice Guy came to the storage building and told me to get up and get in the pickup truck, he was not happy. "I did not know they were going to do this," he confessed. I wasn't sure what he meant or what we were about to do.

He reluctantly started putting the shackles on my wrist and said, "They want me to do this. I have to do it."

I understood. He struggled trying to close the horse-shoe-shaped clasp around my swollen right wrist. My wound didn't really bother me, but those shackles truly hurt. "Those things hurt," I winced.

He stopped for a moment. "I've got to do this," he said sympathetically.

"Just go ahead, I will bear it," I said, wanting him to get it over with.

After squeezing and mashing he got the pin screwed in firmly. My hands began to hurt immediately. He then secured the blindfold and led me to the truck. Wimpy and the guy who did not speak English got in the pickup and we sped down bumpy, crooked roads. We rocked back and forth, which slung my hands from side to side, intensifying the pain. Each hand turned numb.

They were driving unpredictably. We would go a block, take a left, then go another block, and take another left, and then another. It was left, left, left, and right, left, right. We swerved around so much my blindfold came off; it just popped off and sat on top of my head. After about 45 minutes of bouncing around, we pulled up to a tall square building that was about 14 feet high. The structure looked like two large rooms connected by a breezeway of sorts. I later came to call it "The Breezeway House." When we got out of the car, a pack of dogs, maybe a dozen or more, barked loudly about 100 yards away. We walked through a cased opening in the middle of the building, then into a room approximately 15 feet wide by 20 feet long.

Man, I want these shackles off. The intensity of the pain grew by the minute. The lock on the shackles used a small key that went down into the pin to unscrew it. I was worried they were going to lose the key. I would have been in a predicament then.

Another man, whom I had not seen before, walked over to me with the key in hand. He became very frustrated while he tried to take them off. He thought the key only required a half-turn to free the pin. He would turn, then tug and yank on the clamp. He worked away at that shackle without any success. He couldn't get it to do anything, so he walked away leaving the key in place.

I raised my hands to my mouth and clinched the key with my teeth and started twisting to work it around. The man returned and watched. I finally freed the pin and popped the cuff off my right wrist. He came over and removed the other cuff.

They had placed all of my belongings and a pad in the room. They also brought cookies, water, a bottle of Pepsi, and a bottle of some kind of lemon drink. Someone else had seen to it that all of those items were brought along.

One of the men held a lantern up to a window that had been bricked up, pointed to it, and said, "Do not go by this window."

"Okay," I said.

"Do not walk around in here," he added. "If you make noise, we kill you."

A man holding an AK-47 pointed toward the door and said, "Don't go by the door." With that said, they left.

Those guys wanted an excuse to shoot me. They were very serious about their responsibility. I secretly nick-named them "The Guards on Death Row." They were just waiting until my time was up. "Evil" was written all over their shrouded faces. I recited part of the 23rd Psalm to myself, *Yea, though I walk through the valley of the shadow of death, I will fear no evil.*

For some reason the mosquitoes were not as bad at The Breezeway House as they were everywhere else. The pack of dogs barked wildly just outside, and the same kind of crane, or heron-like bird I had heard at The Country Place, made its croaking calls nearby.

They left a lantern in the room, and I left it burning all night. I was able to sleep fairly well, but I either heard or dreamed there were prop-powered aircraft passing some-where in the distance.

CHAPTER
22

MONDAY,
APRIL 26, 2004
IRAQ

THE RABBIT HUNT

The Guards on Death Row arrived at the house about 45 minutes before daylight and escorted me outside to go to the bathroom. We walked about 30 yards before stopping next to a ditch in between some short trees. They allowed me to walk ahead into the bushes leaving them far enough behind that I thought, *It is still dark, and I can probably silently slip through the trees and get several hundred yards away before they realize I'm gone. Then I can run and find a car to hot-wire.* The idea stayed with me only briefly. After considering that I had no idea where I was or how to get to safety, I dismissed the notion just as quickly as I thought about it.

When we got back inside, one of the men handed me a square metal vegetable-oil can approximately 10 inches square and 16 inches tall. The top of the can had been cut out.

He mimicked the act of urinating into it and demanded, "Use this." No doubt, that meant I would be in that room for a long while. They left behind only Pepsi and water to drink.

A breakfast of clabbered milk and bread was waiting on the dirt floor. Still not accustomed to the whole clabbered-milk idea, I lightly dipped the bread into the milk product, even tapped off the excess, and ate mostly bread. The guards watched every bite. After I finished eating, one of the men pointed to his hip then to mine wanting to know if I had given myself a morning shot. I said, "no" and proceeded to mix the saline with the powder. They wanted to watch, so I lowered my pants and injected the medicine.

That set of guards didn't act like they would tolerate much, so I tried to explain my problem with seizures to them. I even acted out a seizure to get them to understand. They said nothing, simply staring at me like I was a man possessed with demons.

Their duties completed, they left for the morning. It wasn't clear where they went or what they did while they were gone. No one stayed there watching or guarding the house between meals or at night. Their day was probably spent at one of the houses down the road. The only reason they returned was to bring food.

Soon after the guards were gone, I began the painful chore of stripping off the old gauze dressing from around my injury. Blotting the area liberally with peroxide was all I could do to treat the wound since the iodine had been left at my last location.

I prepared myself for the day by reciting the 23rd

Psalm quietly, *Yea, though I walk through the valley of the shadow of death, I will fear no evil.*

The room slowly warmed to an angry oven heat. The only ventilation in the room was a tiny hole in the wall, about one inch in diameter, above the bricked-up window. The room was akin to the inside of a car that had been sitting in the sun, with the windows rolled up tight, on a 90-degree Southern summer day. It must have been 120 to 130 degrees in the room most of the day. I was not going to drink the Pepsi. While in training with KBR in Houston, we were taught that caffeine is a diuretic, which removes fluids from the body by making people urinate more than normal, and that can speed up dehydration. I experienced such severe dehydration those first days of captivity that I thought death was imminent. I only drank the water they left behind each day.

I did not want to offend them, though, by not drinking the Pepsi, so I poured some of it into the urine can. Each time they came in they would point to the Pepsi bottle and ask if I was drinking it. I would say "yes." Each morning I would take the can outside and dump its contents into the ditch.

To avoid dehydration I limited my movement and sat on the pad staring at the wall most of the day. With no window or crack in a door to look outside, I became bored stiff. I had to occupy my mind with positive thoughts and not dwell on the heat, The Guards on Death Row, or what was going to happen next.

The dogs barking in the distance reminded me of pleasant days of my childhood. Growing up in the country instilled an appreciation for the outdoors. I learned at an early age to enjoy fishing, hunting, and camping. I had not had the opportunity to hunt in a long time. I had been working too hard and too many jobs to have the time to go. I missed the camaraderie of being with my family and friends, the raw simplicity of a rabbit hunt, the baying of the hounds, and the 10-mile walks.

When I was 10 or 11 years old, my dad, Leo Hamill, would load his beagles into the back of the pickup and take me and my good friend, Steve Allsup, rabbit hunting. Our favorite place to hunt the zigzagging critters was around the swamps adjacent to the Noxubee River. The dogs could always locate plenty of big swamp rabbits to chase. I enjoyed those days and reflected upon one hunt in particular.

I called to mind a crisp winter morning with skies as blue as a bluebird's wings. A faint grayish fog floated eerily above the surface of the swamp. Daddy told Steve and me to take our shotguns, scatter around the thickets, and wait for the dogs to run a rabbit by us.

The wintry air filled my lungs while I hiked into position, clutching the trusty Remington 16-gauge pump shotgun that was as long as I was tall. I was proud of the worn, old shotgun that Daddy passed along to me when he got a new one. Steve and I were a safe distance apart when Daddy turned the pack of beagle hounds loose. Yellow, Sport, Brownie, Sam, and Lady began barking right away as they caught the scent trail left by a swamp rabbit.

When a rabbit is chased by a pack of dogs it runs in a big circle to come back to where it was first jumped. My dad would always bag more rabbits than any of us because he'd follow the dogs until they jumped a rabbit, then wait right there for its return. I wasn't going to let him get the best of me that day. I set up between where the dogs struck, Daddy's standing point, and the barking beagles. I repeated that maneuver over and over effectively cutting Daddy off. As rabbits circled to return to their sanctuary I was there to take them. By the end of the morning I had a half-dozen rabbits hanging around my belt while Dad had none.

I replayed that day a couple of times in my mind, recalling the good times I had with my father, Steve, and the beagles. *When I get out of here I'm going to catch up on the hunting I have missed for so many years*, I promised myself.

As The Guards on Death Row made their way back to The Breezeway House to bring lunch, the bunch of dogs about 100 yards away barked nonstop. The yap of the hounds proved to be an alarm for the movement of the guards. They entered the room carrying a platter filled with rice, cucumbers, tomatoes, and leaven bread. I had been told not to look at the fully masked men, but I managed quick glimpses. They had the look of evil, their stare cut right through me. There was no doubt; they had the will to kill, but no way was I going to show fear. They feed on fear. I was calm and simply ate the food at a normal pace and shoved the plate forward when I was done.

They secured the deadbolt latch on the door and walked away.

An hour or so had passed when I heard the distinct

sound of a turbo-prop C-130 transport aircraft winding up its engines. The medium-range aircraft is proficient at operating from rough, dirt strips and is the prime transport for paratrooper and equipment drops into hostile territories. It can accommodate a wide variety of oversized cargo, including helicopters, six-wheeled armored vehicles, military personnel, and a wide variety of supplies. I figured I must be awfully close to one of our military bases.

I could hear the planes take off, then later land. They were active sporadically all day and into dusk. I felt a confident connection with the familiar sounds of U.S. aircraft and listening to them gave me something to concentrate my mind on during the hot day.

Before the guards arrived with supper, I wanted to give myself the antibiotic vaccination, so I mixed the liquid with the powder and shot it into my left hip. I was so focused on the sounds of the aircraft that I didn't notice the dogs barking, warning of the return of The Guards on Death Row. They abruptly unlocked the door and entered the room with the evening meal, which was the same food as lunch. One of the guards, by way of hand signals, asked if I had given myself the shot. I nodded yes. He must have believed me because they turned and left the room for the evening.

It was becoming evident that their mode of operation was to watch me eat, gather up the waste, ask if I had taken my antibiotic shot, and promptly leave the building. They were consistent with their behavior.

I went to sleep listening to the C-130s lifting off the runway.

CHAPTER
23

**TUESDAY,
APRIL 27, 2004
IRAQ**

AN IMAGE ON
THE WALL

The morning of my nineteenth day of captivity began similar to the days before: a walk to the bushes 45 minutes before daylight. As we made our way back to The Breezeway House I recited the 23rd Psalm to myself, *Yea, though I walk through the valley of the shadow of death, I will fear no evil.*

Breakfast ensued with the customary serving of clabbered milk, bread, and water. After the meal, one of the men whose face was completely wrapped asked, "Have you," gesturing toward his leg as if he was giving himself a shot, "today?" I shook my head no. He started rummaging through my bag, pulled out a vial, handed it to me, and said, "Do it."

The vial read, "Penicillin." A sick feeling washed over

me. I am extremely allergic to penicillin. The last time I took a dose of it I had an adverse reaction. My throat and eyes swelled and I had difficulty breathing. I thought it was going to kill me. It took a trip to the emergency room for an injection to reverse the effect.

They did not understand as I tried to explain why I could not take what was in the vial. The man motioned again toward his leg. He was persistent; I was going to have to give myself the shot regardless. The whole time I was fiddling with the syringe I was silently talking to God:

God, I know what happened the last time I took this medicine. This could be a strong dose, I don't know. I know what penicillin does to me, but I have to give myself this shot. Whatever it does to me you are going to have to take it away. I am not going to be able to get to a doctor like I did the last time.

I prepared the shot and hesitantly gave it to myself. My nose got stuffy and it was a little difficult to breathe, but no other symptoms developed.

The guards left without more ado. Still concerned about a possible reaction to the penicillin, I sat on the pad and took it easy. Plus, they warned me again not to move around or make any noise or I would be killed.

When noon approached, The Guards on Death Row brought another heaping helping of rice, stewed tomatoes, sliced cucumbers, and leaven bread. I ate until I was full, but they insisted, "Eat more." Not wanting to appear disrespectful of their commands, I choked down a little more as they watched every bite. They must have wanted me to stuff myself thinking the nutrition would promote healing in my arm. The four guards picked up the tray and locked the door. The sound of their footsteps faded as they walked to their car.

As I lay there gazing at the far wall, a scene formed. The image appeared as a landscape of trees gently quaking in the breeze. Everything on the wall materialized upside down. I wondered, *How could this be? How can a picture simply show up on this wall?* I was awestruck. I hunted for the source of the image. Light was streaming through the small hole in the opposite wall, much like a movie theater projector, casting the reflection onto the opposite sand-colored wall. Though the image was in color, the colors were not brilliant or saturated. The trees were a muted green and the ground a dull brown.

I later learned this phenomenon is called a "camera obscura" effect. The conditions for this magical event have to be just right. Camera obscura occurs when light travels in a straight line through a tiny hole and some of the rays reflected from a bright subject pass through the hole, traverse, and re-form as an upside-down image on a flat parallel surface. This phenomenon of sunlight only occurs when the hole is very small like the one-inch pinhole in the wall of The Breezeway House. If the hole is too large, an image will not come into focus. Essentially, I was sitting inside a darkened box camera. The outside world was being projected on the dark far wall.

As I sat, leaning against the wall, watching the scene, a

flock of sheep noisily walked by outside, then to my amazement I saw the shadow of a man, his sheep, and a couple of dogs stroll by, upside down. They drifted from left to right along the length of the wall. The shepherd stopped and looked back as though he was looking at me, and then he turned and walked out of the picture.

I did not understand, at the time, how that image was reflected onto the wall. I know how wild it sounds. Perhaps the answer is not complex; maybe it is as simple as answered prayers. There were a lot of things that lifted my faith and spirits and took all doubt away. Even though I viewed The Guards on Death Row as evil and capable of killing me at a moment's notice, I felt a peacefulness surrounding me. There they were telling me I could not look outside, but I had the reflection of the outdoors and the freedom it represented on the wall. They may have shut me in a darkened room with no way to see outside, but God let in the light and that comforting image.

I watched the scene much of the afternoon, marveling: *Maybe this is another sign that God is out there, out in front leading me through this, and wanting me to follow him.*

Time passed swiftly while watching the wonderful "movie" on the wall. About an hour or so before sunset the image faded away.

I must have been so absorbed in the picture show all afternoon that I didn't detect sounds of aircraft. Surely they had been flying all afternoon. As I sat on the pad leaning into the wall I heard a C-130 revving its engines. I listened intently as it took off and made its climb. About

30 minutes later, another plane took off.

Because of the penicillin scare, the image on the wall, and the C-130s, I had neglected my bandage. I painfully stripped away the hardened gauze along with parts of my flesh. The peroxide sizzled and foamed when I dabbed it on the wound's surface. I rewrapped my tortured arm with the white gauze. Not having iodine was troubling, the wound was beginning to drain quite a bit, and I wasn't sure if the antibiotic was the right one for that type of injury.

As dusk approached, I decided to take my evening antibiotic injection before the guards returned. I hoped to avoid running the risk of feeling forced to take another shot of penicillin. Mixing a solution of saline and some sort of antibiotic powder, I noticed the saline was running low. With the powder dissolved, I injected the shot into my left hip.

I heard three more C-130s take off before the barking dogs warned of the four masked men's approach. The sun had been down for an hour by the time they brought in the evening meal of the typical rations. They stood close to the door; one of the men armed himself with an AK-47, which he kept pointed at the floor. Eating in front of that bunch was a bit uncomfortable, but not unnerving. I didn't hurry through the meal nor did I dillydally. If they weren't going to communicate, I wanted them to leave. And, indeed they did.

The occasional barking dog and the distant croaking heron broke the silence of the evening. The C-130 activity increased dramatically later that night. There was one taking off about every 30 minutes. The roar of their engines was consoling music to my ears.

I fell into a deep sleep only to be startled awake by a rustling noise coming from the plastic bag containing my medical supplies. At first I thought it was a mouse, but in that country you never know; it could be any number of undesirable creatures. Carrying the lantern, I walked over to the bag, picked it up, shook it, dug through it, and found nothing. I put it back on the floor and lay down only to have the scratching resume. After two or three times playing that game, I finally surrendered and went to sleep for the night.

An Air Force C-130 Hercules takes off from a military base.

CHAPTER 24

RETALIATION

As the four Guards on Death Row walked me outside, before daylight, to use the bathroom and empty the urine can, I reaffirmed my confidence that I would be released by silently saying a verse from the 23rd Psalm, *Yea, though I walk through the valley of the shadow of death, I will fear no evil.*

It was rather dark, but I looked around at the landscape trying to find the scene that appeared on the wall the day before. I could see an outline of trees that looked similar to the ones I had seen in the image, but it had appeared in my cell upside down and reversed, so it was difficult to identify the exact setting.

When I walked back into the room, I saw where the men had left my bowl of food on the floor, like they were feeding a pet. I slowly ate the usual fare. They talked among themselves while I finished the meal, and they looked on as I mixed the antibiotic solution and injected my left hip.

After the men departed, I prepared to change the dressing on my wound. Every morning I woke to find the gauze embedded in the wound and removing it always proved painful. I clenched my jaw and ripped at the gauze. I soaked three or four cotton balls with peroxide and thoroughly cleaned my wound. It looked awfully bad but had no significant signs of infection. Tissue was continuing to break down and the wound site oozed a watery liquid nonstop. Infection was a real concern because I had no more iodine to treat the area. I wrapped a fresh bandage around the arm knowing the gauze would become fused to the raw, open wound. The following day, regrettably, I would have to repeat the painful procedure.

When The Guards on Death Row, plus a man I didn't recognize, returned with lunch, I had a sense of peace about me that had to be confusing for them. They always studied me and seemed puzzled by my calm demeanor. They could have walked through that door at any moment, taken me outside, and pulled the trigger. The man I had not seen before approached and said, "We have seen pictures of Iraqi men in American prison camps being mistreated by your soldiers. The prisoners were naked, dogs were threatening them, hoods were over their heads, and they were being sexually abused."

"I do not believe that is really happening to your prisoners," I answered in a tone of mistrust. "Americans know full well what that's about. We have had our men mistreated in prisons in past wars. I don't think we would be doing that."

He did not react angrily to my refutation, though he

was obviously upset with the news of the abuse. He just looked at me, took my answer, and left the room along with the other four men. I still did not believe there had been any abuse of Iraqi prisoners but wondered if there would be any retaliation levied against me.

As soon as the men left with the scraps from lunch, I waited for the image on the wall and was not disappointed. It appeared just the same as the day before. The leaves on the trees wobbled in a light breeze and swayed side to side from an occasional gust. On cue, the flock of sheep floated their way across the wall to be followed by the shepherd and his dogs. All the subjects were upside down across the "projection screen." Baaah, baaah bleated the sheep outside the blocked-up window. The shepherd's dogs moved the sheep with soft, short yelps. As the shepherd's likeness was about to disappear, he turned and momentarily looked my way, then stepped from sight. I watched the "movie screen" the rest of the afternoon while the C-130s and an occasional Blackhawk provided the background music.

The panorama of the external world transported me from inside the dark, dreary room and filled me with a great sense of freedom. What a profound phenomenon! The therapeutic value of watching the scene was priceless as it boosted my hope for my own freedom and simply helped me bear the misery of the day. I certainly had no explanation for the occurrence then, but I accepted it, and was soothed with the confidence that the rest of the day would be tolerable. Observing the image, I believe, even helped improve the quality of my sleep at night.

As sunset approached, I rummaged around in the plastic medicine bag and pulled out the last two vials of saline. There was only enough saline and powder for two more injections. I prepared one syringe and shot it into my left hip.

The four Guards on Death Row came back with supper and some extra hardware in the form of shackles and chains. One of them motioned and pointed to his hip wanting to know if I had given myself the shot. I nodded I had.

After I finished the food, one of them shackled my hands first, then knelt down at my feet, spread my legs a little, and wrapped the dog chains tightly around my ankles several times. He ran a bolt through the links to lock them. Each turn of the bolt drew the chain tighter, squeezing off the blood flow to my hands and feet. Satisfied that I was properly trussed, my captors filed out of the room to leave me in agony.

The restraints were enormously painful. The only position that offered relief was to sit in the corner and hold my hands above my head and lean them against the wall. When that grew tiresome, I'd lower my hands and prop my feet up on the adjacent wall.

Between the shackles and chains and mosquitoes there was no way to sleep. Before being shackled I was using the blindfold to swat mosquitoes, but I couldn't even do that with my hands bound. I laid the blindfold across my face for protection, but the buzzing pests would crawl underneath, get on my face, and bite away. Also, later that night the critter returned to the plastic bag and rummaged around for more than an hour. With my hands and feet bound, I could only lie there and listen to its irritating scratching. Sleep was impossible.

That was the first time I wore the shackles all night and the first time they chained my legs. The shackling was in retaliation for the pictures of the Abu Ghraib prisoner abuse they had seen on TV. They chained and shackled me every night afterward.

UH-60 Blackhawk helicopters, such as this, fly support missions for Coalition forces near Baghdad.

CHAPTER
25

THURSDAY,
APRIL 29, 2004
IRAQ

THE BULLY

After a nearly sleepless night and hours of agonizing pain, I was thankful when The Guards on Death Row shuffled into my cell about an hour before sunrise of the twenty-first day of captivity. One of the men, with his face shrouded by his headdress, removed the shackles and chains from my hands and feet and led me outside to relieve myself. As we walked I repeated the verse from the 23rd Psalm in my head, *Yea, though I walk through the valley of the shadow of death, I will fear no evil.* That verse brought me comfort, hope, and confidence that I could face whatever my silent, evil keepers might put me through that day.

They may have ruined my night's sleep with the shackles and chains, but they were going to make sure I was fed. It seemed strange that they could easily put me through a night of torture and then happily give me breakfast. They watched as I dipped the leaven bread into the clabbered-milk concoction and ate until I was overstuffed.

Thank God they did not put the shackles back on. Had I worn them all day it would have been impossible for me to change my bandage, mix the antibiotic, or administer an injection in my hip.

My arm had drained quite a bit during the night and leaked onto the floor in several spots. Each wet area was covered with ants, which were similar in size, but darker than the fire ants we have in Mississippi.

One of the men waved his hand around and pointed at the ants. He left the room for a couple of minutes and returned with a branch from a palm tree. He laboriously swept the floor to create a ball of ants about the size of a softball. He scooped up the scurrying insects in his bare hands and carried them outside.

When he came back he gestured toward my arm as if to say, "Change that bandage." I nodded my understanding. Satisfied with everything, they left me to tend to the wound. My arm had drained a lot during the night, but the dried ooze made it difficult and painful to peel off the gauze. The job had to be completed no matter how much pain I felt, so I ripped the dressing from the raw wound. I dabbed the area with peroxide-drenched cotton balls and watched the bubbling chemical reaction.

The guards were so fixated on the ant problem that they forgot to ask about the shot of antibiotic. I had not forgotten, but I reluctantly retrieved the last syringe of saline and mixed it with the antibiotic powder. Using my injured right arm, I struggled to poke the needle into my right hip to give my other hip a break from the twice-daily shots. I had no iodine and had run out of antibiotics, and my wound was draining more than ever before.

I was dog-tired from lack of sleep the night before and nodded off for a couple of hours only to be roused by the barking dogs, which alerted me to the return of the guards. The Guards on Death Row brought in lunch and an even nastier attitude. Maybe the Abu Ghraib prisoner-abuse incident was on their mind. They were a hard bunch to read because they didn't talk and kept their faces covered. In addition, I didn't look too long at them. The men's eyes were all I ever saw. The brief glances I allowed myself revealed only a distant heartlessness.

I told them I had depleted the saline supply and could no longer mix the antibiotics. They understood me, but it was clear they had no intention of re-supplying the medicine bag. As long as I had medicine, they made sure I used it, but when it ran out, they no longer seemed concerned.

Their routine was always the same: eat and run. They never hung around long, which I definitely preferred over their unpredictable, surly attitudes.

I settled back on the pad and massaged my hands and feet, which were still smarting from a night in shackles and chains. I thought back to a day on the playground of my elementary school. A stereotypical bully had picked on me all year long. We were in the same grade, but he was a lot bigger than everybody else. He amused himself by tripping me or thumping my ears. He was unrelenting, and I just kept taking the abuse.

One day the bully switched targets and picked on a small kid who was a couple of grades below us. I could endure the bully's abuse, but I couldn't stomach watching him pick on someone who had no chance at all of defending himself. No more! I darted up behind him, drove my head between his legs and reared up like a bucking bronco, throwing him headfirst to the ground. I jumped on top of the scoundrel and didn't stop until I had worked him over with some well-placed body punches. That bully never messed with me or anyone else again.

My thoughts returned to the present day and the current conditions our nation faces. Terrorists are the present-day schoolyard bullies. They are bullying America and our allies, and we must stand up to them. On March 11, 2004, Al Qaeda bombed a train in Spain killing 200 people, and they threatened to do more if Spanish troops did not leave Iraq. So Spain made a shameful retreat and handed the terrorist a huge victory. That is what they will repeat in the United States if we don't stand up to them. We must get tougher on them, hit them in the chest with both feet, and not let them up.

The sounds of a C-130 transport airplane interrupted my thoughts and calmed my seething anger. It was impossible to course their direction sitting inside the sealed room. The base could have been north, south, east, or west; I could not tell. I sat, listened, and waited for my late afternoon picture show to begin.

The landscape magically reappeared on the wall. I shifted my weight around, adjusted the pillows, got as comfortable as I could on the thin pad, and watched the movie; the only thing missing was the popcorn. Even though it was a rerun I was still caught up in its majesty. The trees swayed to and fro in the gentle wind. Somewhere around midafternoon and just behind the wall I was leaning against, the shepherd and his flock made their daily trek across the screen. The sheep bleated and the lambs cried. I thought for a moment the shepherd was not going to look back that day, but just before he stepped off the screen he turned and stared in my direction. It was amazing how the images of the outside world brought to me a peaceful sense of freedom and helped pass the time. Before I knew it the afternoon was gone.

Soon after sunset, the massive pack of hounds barked frantically, announcing the coming of the guards. They came into the room still exhibiting the faraway evil look they displayed at lunchtime. I had been at The Breezeway House for four full days at that point and knew it was about time for them to move me to another location. My hope was I'd be moved back to the L-shaped building and stay with Moe, Larry, and Curly. At least they communicated with me and took care of my medical needs. The building had a window, too, which gave me a view of the landscape and some ventilation, as well as a possible means of escape.

The fact that three weeks has passed since I had last taken my seizure medication troubled me. When a seizure hits me, I fall to the floor and lie in a semicomatose state. My eyes are wide open, but I am nonresponsive. I worried that if I had a seizure and The Guards on Death Row tried to make me get up or talk to me, I would only lie there motionless. I was afraid they would consider it disrespectful and possibly shoot me.

There was no hint of a move while the four guards watched me eat my rice, cucumbers, stewed tomatoes, and leaven bread. The food was always the same, but it was good. I enjoyed the meals even with the guards' evil eyes glaring down at me. I have always been able to make do with what I had available. There have been times when all I could afford were hotdogs. I have driven for days across America subsisting on breakfast cereal and truck-stop hotdogs eaten in the solitude of my truck.

Before the men left, they shackled my wrists and chained my ankles. My arm was draining and I wished I had changed the bandage again before the shackles were locked. A clean dressing would have to wait until morning. The shackles and chains were painful and made it tough to sleep, but the calmness I gained by watching the images on the wall earlier in the day made sleep a little easier.

CHAPTER 26

THURSDAY,
APRIL 29, 2004
MACON, MISSISSIPPI

"WE NEED TO GET DNA SAMPLES"

Kellie Hamill had discovered she had an extended family — not just friends, neighbors, and family members in Mississippi, but she had found support from the families of other KBR employees. The mutual support they offered each other helped keep them all emotionally fortified. The one thing each of them wanted to hear was news — something sound, concrete, something they could deal with.

"Every time I turned around someone was over helping do the laundry," Kellie recalled. They would get it all put away, but there would always be one piece of Tommy's clothes left lying around. One sock or a pair of underwear is all it took to make me cry and miss him dearly."

The last thing any of them wanted, other than hearing the worst, was to have additional uncertainty come bearing down upon them. Three weeks after Tommy disappeared, that's exactly what Kellie got.

Starving for new information about her husband's plight, Kellie accepted a telephone call from a sister of one of the KBR drivers. The woman, who chose to remain anonymous, asked if Kellie had been notified about a body, perhaps a fifth KBR employee that had been found in an Iraqi morgue. Apparently, not even the international news media knew about the discovery of the unidentified victim.

"My heart stopped. No one had called to tell me anything like that," Kellie said. "After speaking with that woman, I called KBR and told them I wanted to speak with the most senior official to get the most accurate information they had."

KBR's CEO John Downey took Kellie's call. Trying desperately to maintain her composure, Kellie recalled her training as a 911 dispatcher. She firmly asked for the facts: who, what, where, why, and how.

"I asked them, 'Who dropped the ball? Why was I not notified, and where was the body found?' Up until that point I'd gone with the flow when they [KBR personnel] would call and say, 'Nothing new, no further information.' That was all any of us got. But, I wanted to know why I was not called. Mr. Downey said they just didn't think the body was Tommy."

During her conversation with Downey, another call beeped in on the line. She put Downey on hold and took a call from David Nix, KBR employee assistance program coordinator. "We need to get DNA samples from your

children," he said. "And we need them within 24 hours."
At that point Kellie's world nearly came off the tracks.

"I hung up the phone and told Tommy's mother what
was going on. It was like someone kicked her right in the
stomach; she was going through the same thing I was —
only from the perspective of a mother. I couldn't help but
think, *They know that body is Tommy.*

"As for the DNA, I didn't want to put my kids through
that, so I called Tommy's dad and asked him if he would
provide a DNA sample, and he agreed."

Flooded with questions and no answers and already
desperately clinging to hope, the news of an unidentified
body blindsided Kellie. On top of that, the request for
DNA compelled her to think the worst had happened.
The entire chain of events, three weeks after Tommy disappeared, proved to be one of the most trying times for
her during the whole ordeal.

Later, Kellie learned that the unidentified body was not
an American. The news, however, provided only a little
relief as the dread of thinking the worst reverted back to
the aching anxiety of uncertainty.

During her long days Kellie tried to do little things that
kept Tommys presence around the house.

"I even took his favorite cologne and sprayed just
enough on his pillow to remind me of him," Kellie
recalled. "It helped me rest and gave me a secure feeling.
Actually, Tori did that before I did. It is amazing that a little 12 year old girl would think of such, but, like me, she
wanted that feeling of her Dad being close by."

Kellie and Tommy pose with their children in a 1993 photograph. Kellie was alarmed by a request from KBR for a DNA sample from the children that might be required to identify Tommy's remains.

THE EIGHTH-GRADE PROM

The dogs began their annoying barking, signaling the morning arrival of The Guards on Death Row. The longer I remained in the care of that bunch, the more I was convinced that they possessed both the will and determination to kill me. They never talked with me, and as ordered, I did not look directly at them. All they needed was some obscure motive to shoot me. I could not dwell on those thoughts. Instead, I repeated; *Yea, though I walk through the valley of the shadow of death, I will fear no evil.* That psalm and prayer was the only thing that gave me hope that I'd live through it all.

I looked away as the four guards delivered breakfast. They stood against the far wall talking to each other and clutching their AK-47s. When I finished eating the clabbered milk and bread, the guards collected the remains and left the room.

My wound had drained a lot during the night, leaving wet areas on the dirt floor. Ants covered each damp spot. The maid service from the day before didn't continue for a second day. I moved my pad away from the ants and the puddles on the floor, and began unwrapping my bandages.

Soaking several cotton balls with peroxide, I patted the injury site. With no iodine to treat the area, I simply enveloped the wound with numerous wraps of gauze. I stuffed the gore-soaked bandages into one of the plastic bags that served as the trash container. I needed another antibiotic shot, but the saline was gone.

At that point in my captivity, I had totally lost track of time. One of the last times I had talked with my family, Thomas, my son, told me he was excited about attending the eighth-grade prom, scheduled for April 24. I thought it had to be close to or past that date. I sat there worrying about him. I was afraid the trauma of my capture might shut him down emotionally and keep him from attending.

When I went home for Kellie's surgery, I had a father-son chat with Thomas, who was 13 at the time, about the prom. He was excited about asking Kindra Hines, a beautiful 16-year-old girl, to be his date. He was nervous but finally asked her to go with him, and she accepted. When I was his age I couldn't even muster the courage to ask any girl out. I was proud that he felt confident enough to ask a young lady three years his senior.

Up to that point, I had not fretted over what might have been happening back home. But that prom was very important to him; therefore, it was important to me. He would have only one opportunity to attend an eighth-grade prom, and I hoped he would go and enjoy it.

The days seemed to drag on forever in The Breezeway House. No one talked to me, or even prayed in front of me, to break up the monotony. There were no windows to gaze through or even any lizards to keep me company, only four walls, a few plastic bags, a pad, two pillows, and a urine can. There was too much time to sit, think, and worry.

I fought the temptation to wallow in pity or worry over matters I could not control. It would have been easy to sit there and become a total nut case. I had already prayed to God to take care of everything, to take away the worry and fear. I didn't have to pray the same prayer every day over and over again. God knew what I needed (he heard the first prayer), but I prayed often and recited verses from the Bible to help pass the time and to reaffirm my total dependence on him to get me through.

The dogs barked their warning, and I knew The Guards on Death Row were returning. The four of them entered the room with stoic expressions and lunch. They looked on as I ate the rice, cucumbers, and stewed tomatoes, and drank the bottled water. They didn't talk, not even to each other. I quickly finished the meal, not because I was that hungry but to give them a reason to leave.

One of the men noticed the ants crawling around on the floor and ordered one of the others to go outside. The fellow returned with a frond from a palm tree, handed it to me, and pointed toward the ants. I swept ants, using my good left arm, from all over the room. One of the guards kept pointing to more ants, the ones I had missed. I fought through the pain in my right arm, worked harder to sweep up all the insects, and at last built a pile about the size of a grapefruit. One of the men came over, bent down, scooped up the mound in his hands, and ran it outside. The housekeeping complete, the guards left for the afternoon.

Not long after their departure, the upside-down scene on the far wall developed and helped occupy my mind. The green leaves trembled in the slight wind. Eventually, the sheep filed into the frame, and then the shepherd appeared behind them. They flowed across the wall in slow motion. The shepherd's white robe fluttered in the breeze as he moved from left to right. He looked back as if he were looking at me and then disappeared. Perhaps he was looking for a lost lamb or making sure his dogs were still following, but he appeared to be looking straight at me. Not only did the scene help pass the time, but it also conveyed a sense of peace and comfort that helped me deal with all of the uncertainty of being held prisoner.

I catnapped off and on throughout the afternoon and the C-130s droned intermittently. Twilight came and it wasn't long before the pack of dogs started barking. The four men entered the room with a tray full of food expecting me to eat it all. I was hungry and ate until I was overstuffed.

Soon, the men gathered the leftovers, shackled me, and left. I sat on the pad, leaned against the wall, and listened to the C-130 transport planes take off. The engines' pitch would alter as the big planes gained altitude. I could not

229

determine from which direction the planes were starting or which way they were headed. At times it seemed like they were circling overhead. Later, a couple of Blackhawk helicopters circled overhead and then swept the area.

There was a flurry of military-aircraft activity that night, but none of them fired any rounds. It was heartening to know our military was nearby and that a base was close at hand. I was so worn out that even with the shackles, I managed intermittent sleeping spells throughout the night.

Thomas with his date, Kindra Hines,
at the eighth-grade prom.

CHAPTER
28

SATURDAY,
MAY 1, 2004
IRAQ

EVE OF
FREEDOM

The Guards on Death Row were again prompt on the morning of my twenty-third day of captivity. They arrived at what I perceived to be the same time every morning and then busied themselves with the chores associated with starting my day. They first removed my shackles, then led me on a walk in the dark to the outdoor bathroom. Then, they served me the usual breakfast.

As soon as they walked out of my cell, I began changing the bandage covering my wound. It was a mess. I grew more concerned about my wound. It drained more each day, and the lack of iodine and antibiotic spelled trouble. If I didn't get help soon, I could lose my arm or die from infection.

Though I had repeated the verse from the 23rd Psalm for the past several days, it had not gotten mundane; *Yea, though*

I walk through the valley of the shadow of death, I will fear no evil. Those words provided the peace my soul needed and enabled me to have a settled mind, which I would need in case God provided a way for me to escape.

I had been held at The Breezeway House for six days, which was two more days than I expected. I felt it was only a matter of time before they moved me elsewhere. The Nice Guy had told me that they moved me around frequently to avoid the U.S. Military patrols. Since I was held close to an air base, I was surprised that they had kept me in The Breezeway House as long as they had.

My days were numbingly routine, but I felt thankful that I didn't have to wear the shackles during the day. Without the restraints I was able to change my bandage and nap more comfortably.

My personal movie began again when the sun rose high enough to create the spectacular, upside-down phenomenon. The trees shuddered and quaked in the breeze. I watched, thankful for its daily arrival. The vision of the outside world filled the afternoons and helped prevent any worry that might have occupied my mind otherwise. The shepherd and his flock appeared on cue for their stroll across the wall. Never in a hurry, they seemed to measure each step. Remarkably, the man looked back toward me for the fifth straight day. Regardless of how this phenomenon may be explained, it served me well and brought a comforting peace that I may not have found without it. The motion picture played most of the afternoon, fading from view about an hour before the last light of day.

But then I suddenly felt weak, like I was about to collapse. I sat down on the pad. The room spun wildly. My equilibrium was way off. My ears began ringing. I worried I was about to have a seizure, and I knew the guards were due back soon.

Slowly the symptoms subsided and I returned to normal. I knew I could not stop a seizure and that one could put me out at anytime. I just hoped, if one did occur, The Guards on Death Row would not be around to witness it.

The drone of the big C-130 engines that continued throughout the afternoon provided a transition from the close of day to the beginning of night. I passed several more hours alone and unfed, since the guards were running late. *Something's up*, I told myself.

It must have been around 11 that night when the dogs finally cranked up. Soon an older, barrel-chested guy (whom I had not seen before), Wimpy, a young teenage boy, and The Guards on Death Row walked through the door. One of the guards attached the shackles, blindfolded me, and guided me to a pickup truck. I could not tell who got in the truck with me, but there were two of them. I sat in the middle with my left leg resting against the gearshift. We rode for about 45 minutes to a new site.

When the two men talked to each other, I thought the passenger sounded like he might be Wimpy. When we parked, sure enough, Wimpy removed my blindfold and then the shackles. The driver was a 30-something-year-old man, another new player in the game of "hide the prisoner." With my eyes uncovered, I saw the barrel-chested man and the teenage boy standing outside the truck. Since it was not physically possible to transport all five of us in the cab of the truck, the barrel-chested man and the teenager either rode in the back of the truck or arrived at the new location ahead of us.

The 30-year-old man turned the truck around and backed close to a ditch. When they lowered the tailgate, it created a bridge over the trench. Wimpy pointed and commanded me to "walk" toward an old mud hut a few yards away. They walked with me, and a serious discussion in Arabic, complete with ominous tones, ensued.

The building's southern and western walls were marred with cracks and holes. The door was long gone, with only a cased opening remaining. I took a seat outside the hut as instructed. They continued their conversation. It was at least midnight and maybe later. The moon was practically full and lit up much of the countryside.

Wimpy asked, "Are you hungry? Do you want something to eat?"

"Yes, I could eat a little something." I replied. Actually I was very hungry.

Wimpy walked down to a big house that was just in front of the hut. About 15 minutes later he came back with a huge tray of cucumbers sliced lengthwise, stewed tomatoes, and bread. Everyone sat on the ground as we ate our picnic by moonlight. There was no friendly after-dinner conversation. The old barrel-chested guy and Wimpy spoke to each other in Arabic. The old barrel-chested guy hugged his AK-47 like an old friend. The rifle's butt rested on the ground as he wrapped one arm around the forestock while leaning the barrel against his shoulder.

Since I couldn't understand what they were saying, I didn't pay much attention. I stared at the lights glistening in the distance. There were a series of red lights near the ground, and I wondered if that was a landing strip near Baghdad. The moon was so bright I could see for miles. We were in an agricultural area; plowed fields surrounded us. Then, behind the mud hut, I saw the moonlight reflecting off a large lake and noticed irrigation ditches fanning out in several directions.

The old barrel-chested guy and Wimpy got my attention when they got louder. I looked on as they passed the AK-47 back and forth. They were arguing about who would take the gun for some reason. It was for all the world like two kids fighting over a toy.

Wimpy gained control of the gun and held it tightly as they both walked over to me. Wimpy asked, "Do you want to sit, walk, stand, or what?"

"I'll just stay seated," I answered not understanding the point of the question.

"Well get up," Wimpy demanded.

He walked me around to the backside of the building, and Wimpy, the 30-year-old, and I stumbled through the night. I became suspicious. *He's going to walk me away from the building out into the night, shoot me, drive off, and leave me right here.*

I mentally countered, *Well, why did they feed me if they have plans on killing me?*

I chastised myself for allowing my mind to lead me somewhere else and not placing the situation in God's hands.

The 30-year-old reached down and picked up an old piece of plywood as we continued to walk. Wimpy was acting nutty. The whole time we were walking he was taking dry aim with his AK-47. He fell into the prone shooting position, lying on his stomach with both of his elbows planted firmly on the ground, and aimed the rifle out into the open farm fields. Next, he got up, went to a tree, and acted like he was hiding. Then he placed the barrel of the AK-47 across a limb while he took aim. Playing out his macabre "army-man" game, he took a standing position, placing the butt of the gun to his shoulder first, then resting the forearm of the stock on top of his hand to aim.

We walked over a bank and across an irrigation ditch. The 30-year-old laid the plywood on the ground and told me to sit on it. Wimpy kept walking around shouldering his gun, practicing, and acting crazed. Then he began walking in circles around me gripping his gun. *This is it,* I thought to myself. *If this is the way my life is to end, I am ready.* I prayed:

God I am not going to question this. I don't want to die here. I have a family. I want to go home to them. I know they will be devastated if I die here. If I am to die here, then I am ready to die here. I lay it all at your feet. I lay it all at the cross.

Wimpy swiftly walked down to where the old barrel-chested guy was standing and talked to him for a minute.

I figured the old man was asking him what he was waiting for or why he hadn't heard a shot yet. Wimpy came back and started walking around me again still holding the gun. Then all of a sudden he demanded, "Get up, we are going back to the house."

What a relief, to say the least. But, what was the purpose of that 45-minute episode? Was it mental torture? Could Wimpy not muster up the courage to shoot me? Or, did God lay his hand on those men's hearts? It was all out of my control. God had taken all of the confusion and worry away.

As we walked back to the hut, I noticed the holes in the southern and western walls had been filled with wet mud. A big piece of sheet metal had been leaned up against the door opening. The four men began preparing the inside of the hut by bringing in a sheet of plastic to cover the floor. They also brought a pad, my medicine bag, some water, and some cookies. I wondered, *Did Wimpy and the 30-year-old walk me back there so the other two could patch the building, or did they instruct Wimpy to shoot me and he just couldn't do it?* Regardless of what had just happened, I didn't question the result, and all I could say, over and over, was "Thank you, God."

The mosquitoes were horrible, due to all of the water in the irrigation ditches. Hundreds of the pesky insects were already on the attack. Wimpy, the old barrel-chested guy, the 30-year-old, and the teenager walked outside taking the lantern with them, leaving me in total darkness. They propped the piece of sheet-metal up against the door opening and jammed something tightly against it.

They talked for a while, and then it became silent outside. I felt sure they were still out there but had fallen asleep. Crawling sounds from the night creatures intensified from the floor and walls. Vipers hang out around water, and we were close to lots of it. Though it was cool, I didn't cover up with the blanket because snakes look for warm places at night, and I did not want to wake up eye to eye with one coiled on my chest.

I stayed awake all night. Between the darkness, buzzing, biting mosquitoes, and slithering crawlers, sleep was out of the question. Even though they did not shackle me, there was too much going on in that room to fall asleep. By morning I was beat.

*The mud hut near Balad where Tommy spent his last night
before escaping through the door on the left.*

Tommy's sleeping quarters inside the mud hut.

CHAPTER
29

SUNDAY,
MAY 2, 2004
IRAQ

THE GREAT
ESCAPE

Days turned into nights. Nights turned into days. In between, simple tasks such as eating, drinking, sleeping, urinating, and defecating, all under the watch and at the convenience of people who wished me harm, had begun to blur the distinctions that separate parts of the day. Blindfolds and chains had begun to take away my ability to orient myself with the places in Iraq I had come to know. It took only three weeks to begin to feel lost in space and time. Still, I tried to be resilient and ever hopeful; I had to be. I did not dwell on thoughts that might prove fruitless. Ready to go home, I was resigned to accept either destination God would choose: heaven or the nearest thing to heaven on earth — Macon, Mississippi.

Similar to the way The Guards on Death Row treated

242

me, Wimpy, the old barrel-chested guy, and the young kid stumbled in to wake me and walked me, like a dog, outside to relieve myself 45 minutes before daylight. They allowed me to walk around behind the building while they lingered out front. I could see well enough to study the area in more detail than I could the night before, but it was still fairly dark. I tried to figure out where we were, but nothing provided a clue.

I trudged back inside the building. One of the men wedged the metal door shut and all was quiet again. The rising sun drove the mosquitoes out of my cell after they had spent the night dining on my blood. I was exhausted by lack of sleep. I rolled over on my pad and was dead to the world in a matter of seconds.

Three, maybe four hours later I woke up. There was finally enough light outside that I got my first glimpse at the inside of my new surroundings. The low ceiling was made of mud packed between stick rafters. Unlike my other prisons, which were made of block, the walls of the hut had been made of packed mud and a wooden framework. The ceiling bore signs that it just managed to shield its previous occupants from the weather. Old water stains streaked down the wall and met an eroded trench that ran across the floor.

I was a little hungry and wondered why Wimpy and the men hadn't brought breakfast. They had left behind a package of cookies and some water, so I began eating. As I munched the cookies I heard a familiar sound outside, but I kept eating. The noise kept getting louder. *That's something I have not heard recently. That's a diesel engine or a*

Humvee motor clattering. That's either a Humvee or a 5-ton!

I jumped up, ran over to the door and pushed it with my left shoulder. The door moved only a tiny bit but enough that I could see out. There were three or four tandem-axle, 5-ton Army trucks with a Humvee in the lead and one in the rear. U.S. troops were walking in front of, behind, and alongside the convoy as it slowly moved in my direction.

I thought, *Maybe this is God's way of letting me know that there is no way these troops are going to be able to load up and leave before I can get to them, like what happened on the day when I was captured.*

I pushed on the door, but it wouldn't move an inch. Then, I got a good grip on the sheet metal and pulled and tugged with my entire might. It slid to one side creating a V-shaped opening that I thought might be just big enough to crawl through. I knew there was a guard outside, and he would shoot me if I ran out. He would have time to kill me and disappear before the soldiers could react. I prayed:

God, you are going to have to take care of that guard because I am not going to wait. I am going to run over to those soldiers. I am going to them.

I pressed my body against the metal door and pushed and squeezed until I popped through to the outside. I did not see anyone and took off running, kicking my sandals off as I ran across an open rocky field. The troops were a good half-mile away and I wasn't sure at what point they would be able to hear me, but I started hollering as loud as I could, "I'm an American! I'm an American!" I stripped off my shirt as I ran barefoot across a rocky plowed field. I wanted them to see that I was white and that I was not some crazy person running at them with bombs strapped to me. I waved my black shirt as I ran past people working in the fields on both sides of me.

I felt like I needed to let the soldiers know I was wounded or in distress, so I just stumbled and fell over. I got up, ran a few more steps, stumbled, and fell again. I looked up and saw that they had stopped and were all staring at me. I then started yelling again, "I'm an American P.O.W.! I'm an American P.O.W.!"

Some of the soldiers in the middle column started walking toward me. That's when I knew the ordeal was over.

They did not recognize me at first. Out of breath, happy, and relieved, I said, "I am Thomas Hamill. I am the KBR employee who was captured on April 9th."

"We know who you are now," said one of the soldiers. "We've seen pictures of you at our briefings. You were kidnapped."

I pointed at the building I had just run from, "I came from that house over there."

"That house right there?" a soldier asked pointing to the big house in front of the mud hut I had just escaped from.

"No, not the big house, the little one behind it."

They immediately sent a patrol over to investigate. In the meantime, they brought a medic to examine me. I told him that I was fine; I just wanted something to drink.

"I don't need anything from that bag; my bandage is

fine just the way it is. I will tend to it when we get to wherever we are going. I would just like some water."

The medic gave me a bottle of water and asked, "Do you want any food?"

"No, just water. I want to get somewhere and call my wife. Where are we anyway?"

"We are about 20 to 30 miles west of Balad, just north of Baghdad," answered one of the soldiers. "We are trying to get a Medivac helicopter in here to pick you up." I thought we would probably go to a nearby camp at Balad, and there, I could call Kellie to let her know I was safe.

Another soldier told me they were the 2nd Battalion, 108th Infantry from a New York National Guard unit. One of them said they had gotten up early that morning to pull security for a crew while they worked on a ruptured pipeline that had been blown up. "These are the coordinates we were given right in this area, but we haven't seen a pipeline that has been blown up," he said. "That's probably where we are supposed to be," pointing to a plume of black smoke some seven or eight miles away.

It was about 11 in the morning when the patrol came back from the house. One of the soldiers was carrying the AK-47 Wimpy had paraded around with the night before. He said he found the gun laying on the ground behind the mud hut. He also said they had detained two men and were interrogating them in front of the big house.

One of the soldiers said they had just walked by the mud hut a few moments earlier. I must have been asleep because I hadn't heard anything. I thought, *That's how God took care of that guard. If those soldiers had not walked by that hut earlier, the guard would have been there when I broke out. He could have shot me and gotten away before anybody could have caught him. When he heard the soldiers coming, he probably just laid down his gun and walked away as if he was a local farmer. He might even have walked right past the soldiers.*

I did not recognize the two men they were questioning in front of the big house, but I bet they knew about me. The food we ate came from that house. The patrol searched the house and didn't find anything inside to cause them to arrest the two men, but they weren't done with them.

Meanwhile, the patrol was trying to send our location from the Humvee to the Medivac helicopter. A soldier said it would be an hour before they could get to us, so I got into the back of a 5-ton truck. We drove up to the house and some of the soldiers took pictures of the mud hut and a few shots of me in front of it. A soldier took off his flak vest, put it on me, and I went down and sat next to one of the irrigation ditches. I watched the military guys continue questioning the two men. A woman, who was in the house, ran outside yelling and waving her arms, apparently offended by the soldiers being in her house.

But about 12:30, I could hear the helicopters approaching. Using a smoke flare the soldiers lit as a guide, the two Medivac helicopters circled then landed. A three-man crew helped me aboard and strapped me in one of the helicopters. I waved happily to the soldiers and gave them a thumbs-up as we lifted off the ground.

"Are we going to Balad?" I asked a crew member.

"No. We've got orders to fly you to Tikrit," he answered.

I knew that was up north and much farther away. I asked, "Can't we just go to Balad? It's closer. I want to call my wife."

Then a thought flashed in my mind, *You are free, just relax and go wherever they say.*

"I'm sorry. Tikrit will be fine," I said before they had a chance to respond.

The helicopter ride to Tikrit lasted about 45 minutes. I was ushered into a field hospital where several doctors examined my wound and took X-rays. Two men from a contract security firm walked in with weapons. The doctors told them to get out, but they said they were not going anywhere, because they had been sent to protect me and weren't leaving. The doctors said they couldn't be there with loaded weapons, but, of course, the security team refused to unload. They weren't going to lose me again.

After the doctors finished their exam, the security folks began asking me a lot of questions. They wanted to know if I knew the locations where I had been held. Then they showed me photographs of the men in my convoy who were found dead and said that two were still missing. They had several pictures of all the men in my convoy and wanted to know if I knew them. I said that I knew all of them.

They told me Matt Maupin, a soldier in our convoy, was being held hostage. I told them about Snappy telling me they had a soldier they were holding.

I still had not called Kellie so I asked again if I could

call her. Someone brought a satellite phone. I walked outside and punched in the number I had wanted to call for more than three weeks. It was about 3:30 or 4:00 in the afternoon Iraq time, or 6:30 or 7:00 in the morning in Mississippi. When Kellie answered, I said, "Hey baby. I'm okay and I'm coming home."

To say that Kellie was excited is an understatement. She told me KBR had already called and informed her that I had escaped. I told her, "I have been worried about you the whole time." I was concerned about how she was doing in the aftermath of her surgery and coping with my capture. She assured me she was doing fine now. I asked, "Did Thomas go to the prom?" She said Thomas did go to the prom and had a good time, and also that Lewis Bailey, an NBC news cameraman, tagged along and got it all on video for me. She wanted to know how I was doing and when I would be coming home. I told her I was first going to Germany and that I would call and give her more details later.

Two Blackhawk helicopters arrived, picked me up, and flew me to BIAP where a psychiatrist and an investigator were waiting in a big military tent. I am sure the psychiatrist thought, "This guy is going to be a nut case; not being a soldier, not having the training, and being a hostage for 24 days, he's going to be crazy."

I detailed the 24 days and told him, "I'm not going to have a problem with any of this. I just want to get back to my family. Let me see my wife. I am totally fine."

He talked with me about the places I had been held and

told me they had people looking for me every day. I told them everything I could remember. The investigator said that the information I provided would be of considerable help with other hostage situations.

The investigator said, "I am supposed to fly with you to Germany; that's part of my job. But I am not going to have to go with you. You're not going to have any trouble."

I think they were both amazed that I was not having any emotional difficulties and that my capture would have no residual effects on my mental health.

The investigator showed me several photographs of known insurgents. I identified two of them. One was Tiger, the man who stole my wedding ring. I recognized him right away. The other was the man who wore the red headdress and claimed I was a soldier during the questioning at the L-shaped building. I had seen just enough of his eyes and his hawkish nose to know without a doubt he was the one in the photograph.

The military folks were so good to me. They served me a steak and vegetables, which I thoroughly enjoyed. I got to take a lengthy, hot shower. It felt so good to get cleaned up and wear my own fresh clean clothes, which they had retrieved from Camp Anaconda.

A KBR official on the scene asked if there was anybody I wanted to accompany me to Germany. I said, "I have a good friend, Mark Lee, who is over here, but I don't know where he is today. I don't know whether he's on a mission or not. If you can get him to go with me that would be great."

In a little while, the psychiatrist came in the tent and said they had found Mark. He told me to expect Mark to arrive sometime that night or the next morning.

I was free, clean, well fed, and got to sleep on a real bed for the first time in 24 days. My feet were beat-up and bruised from running barefooted across the jagged rocks in the field, but if that's the cost of freedom, I will gladly pay it every time.

Troops from the 2nd Battalion, 108th Infantry, New York National Guard escort Tommy away from the mud hut.

*Tommy gives a thumbs-up with his freshly bandaged
arm seated beside a well-armed guardsman from the patrol
who discovered him near Balad.*

*A Medivac helicopter lands to pick up
Tommy after his escape.*

CHAPTER
30

AFTERMATH

President Bush learned of Hamill's escape Sunday morning. "It's great news for all Americans, and the president is happy for Mr. Hamill and family," White House spokeswoman Erin Healy said.

A Chinook helicopter delivered Mark Lee that morning. I shared with him the events of the past 24 days. I asked him about some of the other guys who were in my convoy, but regretfully he didn't know much. He did say that after the attack, several of them had quit and gone home.

Late that morning a Blackhawk helicopter picked us up and flew us to Camp Anaconda in Balad. I wanted to see some of my buddies at the camp, but we set down on the landing strip and they were all on the other side of the compound. Mark and I waited at the terminal for the C-

141 transport plane that would take us to the Ramstein Air Base in rural western Germany.

We boarded the plane and were waiting for a couple of soldiers who were in such bad shape that the medical staff didn't want to board them until the last possible second. Mark and I sat in jump seats along the wall. The scene inside the plane shocked me. It was like a trip back in time. The plane's interior resembled an old one-room hospital ward except the gurneys were stacked three high, one on top of another, and suspended from the ceiling by heavy-duty straps. There were at least a dozen wounded soldiers, some were not moving while others remained alert but suffering from wounds to their legs or arms. The medics kept asking if I wanted to lie down on a gurney. I didn't feel worthy enough to get onto one of the gurneys alongside all of those soldiers with much worse injuries than mine. Somehow I did not feel like I deserved to be there with them, but I considered it an honor to be on the same flight with those 20- to 21-year-old men who were sacrificing their bodies and lives to do their duty. Some folks have called me a hero, but those brave men are the true heroes. My hat is off to each one of them and my prayers go out to them and their families.

One of the medics eventually took a back support off of a gurney, attached it to some hanging straps against the wall. I laid down on it and he strapped it onto the board for the rest of the flight.

Some of the soldiers with critical wounds were attached to heart monitors, beeping their own distinct chirps, that looked like computer screens. Their screens flashed with blue, green, and red lights. Respirator's constant, soft whistles echoed throughout the ward. Blood pressure cuffs hissed as they expanded and contracted at irregular intervals. Each man had two or three IV lines plugged into his hands, arms, and neck. Some had oxygen monitors that sounded a loud, insistent alarm when detached from the patient's finger during care.

Four medics, two men and two women, were constantly attending to the soldiers' needs, checking the doctors' orders on the charts, and recording the vital signs of the wounded men.

The excitement of being free and heading home was tempered by the somber mood on board as the gurneys swayed and creaked with the motion of the plane. The five-hour flight to Ramstein Air Base allowed me time to reflect upon the power of prayer and how truly grand it is that God listened to one man and worked a miracle for me and my family.

I was told the media would be waiting for my arrival, but the pilot pulled the plane away from where the media had gathered. An Army bus whisked me away to the U.S. military's Landstuhl Regional Medical Center.

I was placed in a treatment room and greeted by Air Force psychologist Colonel Sally Harvey. Soon, Major Kerry Jepsen, an Air Force doctor, came in to examine my arm. He said the work of the Iraqi doctors was consistent with treatment of the wound and that X-rays revealed the bullet shattered the ulna bone in my right forearm.

Doctor Jepsen had been told to expect a patient with an open gunshot wound and was expecting the affected area to be infected. He was amazed that there was no sign of infection given my dirty living environment. He prescribed an antibiotic treatment and said I could wait until I got home to get further care. Doctor Jepsen asked if there was anything I wanted, something that I may have particularly missed while I was being held hostage. I asked for a burger, fries, and a Coke.

A neurosurgeon also stopped by to talk with me about my seizure disorder and checked my medication blood level. Everything seemed to check out okay.

Later in the day Colonel Harvey came to my room to tell me that Kellie would be flying over to be with me. That was good news, something I looked forward to with great anticipation.

She also said that Arnold Schwarzenegger was at the hospital visiting the troops and wanted to pay me a visit. She asked if I would like to meet him. I said I would like to meet him, but only if he did not bring his press crew or any cameras. She went down, talked with him, and came back to report he had agreed to come alone to see me.

Governor Schwarzenegger came in and stayed about five minutes. He said, "I want you to know we support you and wish you the best of luck. You are a brave man. It must be unbelievable to face the threat of dying every day." I enjoyed our brief visit and was honored to meet him. Without the cameras and press crew, he was an ordinary man, and that's what I wanted. He seemed very genuine.

Earlier in the day Schwarzenegger addressed hundreds of troops. "I have been all over the world," he told the crowd. "It (the United States) is without any doubt the best place in the world. We have the mightiest military. We have the greatest economy, but how did we get to that power? The way we got there is by continuously protecting what we have. You are the ones who have helped."

The bodybuilder-turned-actor-turned-governor stirred the spirits of the soldiers when he stated, "I play the Terminator. I play the commando, but you are the true action heroes."

I addressed the media on Tuesday, May 4th by saying, "I am very glad to be back on an American installation. I look forward to returning to America.

"First and foremost I would like to thank the American public for their support of all deployed in the Middle East. Please keep your thoughts and prayers with those who are still there."

"I am feeling well and have few problems with my injury. I would like everyone to know I have received good care and am looking forward to reuniting with my wife in the morning and thank you so very much and God Bless."

I went through a debriefing process or repatriation, as the military calls it, which included talking with the U.S. Air Force SERE (Survival, Evasion, Resistance, Escape) specialists for a few hours each day for three or four days. There were five different guys I talked with. They wanted

me to tell them everything that happened from the attack
to my escape. They recorded the interviews and took lots
of notes. I provided as much detail as I could remember.
When we finished they said, "We don't know how you
did it. You aren't a soldier, and you haven't been trained.
We have a book we go by, we train by this book. You
don't have the book, yet you did everything right in line
with its instructions."

"God got me through this, I followed His book," I
said. "He got me through this from day one through
twenty-four." I could tell that those guys were Christians
too. Some of them got teary-eyed when I mentioned that
I believed God had taken care of me.

Kellie Goes Shopping

One of the first things Kellie noticed about Tommy was
that he wasn't wearing his wedding ring. He shared the
story about how one of the captors had taken it off his finger. "That ring was sacred," Kellie said. "It was ours. Sure,
we could replace the ring, but it hurt; it just ate at me."

While Tommy went through the repatriation process, a
soldier named Jason, was assigned to help Kellie with
anything she needed. Wanting to prepare Tommy a home-
cooked meal, Jason escorted Kellie to the PX to pick up
some steaks, potatoes, and the fixings to make a choco-
late cake. While there they passed a jewelry counter.

"I had no intention of purchasing anything, but I was
curious and asked Jason if we could just look for a
minute," Kellie said. "As soon as we stepped inside, I saw

a set of wedding bands that tore at my heart. The matching gold bands had a leaf on each side of a heart with a cross inside the heart. The salesperson said they were the only set like them they had. I didn't want to spend the money, I didn't even know if they would fit, so I talked myself out of looking any further.

"We left and continued our walk, circling back around, passing the jewelry counter again. Something was drawing me toward that counter, so I had another look. The salesperson said the man's ring was size ten-and-a-half and the woman's was six-and-a-half. I normally wear a seven and had no idea what size Tommy wore. I asked if they had a means of sizing that I could somehow sneak onto Tommy's finger to measure his size. She said no. Then I asked if they could resize them, and again no was the answer. Once again, I talked myself out of the notion of buying the rings."

Kellie and her escort finished their grocery shopping. "Those rings kept pulling me back like a magnet," Kellie said. "I asked Jason if we could go back one more time. He agreed. We went back to the counter, and I told the lady I wanted the rings. The clerk said if the rings didn't fit, they could not be returned. The clerk asked, "Do you know what these rings mean?"

"I have no idea," Kellie answered.

"The leaf on the side is the leaf of hope, the heart is for love, and inside the heart is a cross, which is for Christ," she said. That sealed the deal for Kellie.

Colonel Harvey was like a mother to me. I don't know what I would have done without her. She knew my needs before I did. I didn't have to ask for anything, she understood what I had been through and knew how to deal with it. She walked me to get a haircut and to get the hamburger I had requested. I kept reassuring her that I had already made my peace with God about all that happened and that I was not going to come home any less of a man than when I went over there. They were not going to have to worry about me cracking up over the ordeal.

Colonel Harvey told me Charlie Daniels was at the hospital. He had just performed a concert for the troops. I have always been a fan of the Charlie Daniels Band and told her I would like to meet him. She said he and his band were about to leave, and we would not have time to see them.

Later in the afternoon Colonel Harvey came by my room and asked if I wanted to take a walk. I had been cooped up in that room, so I was ready to go. The five SERE specialists joined us as we walked the grounds of the hospital. Colonel Harvey pointed out the Fisher House where families of patients reside while their loved ones are being treated. She said Kellie would be staying there and that I would probably be moved there with her for a few days to get readjusted to family life. As we continued our walk, a man with the media spotted us, turned, and ran back to his truck for his camera. Colonel Harvey said, "We are going to have to make an about-face." By the time he got his camera, we were gone.

We made a left turn, then a right, and were heading back to the main building when I noticed the bus for the Charlie Daniels Band. Charlie was standing outside doing an interview. Colonel Harvey asked if I wanted to try to meet him, and I said, "Sure." She went down and talked to his PR person. She came back and told me that he wanted to come up to meet me.

I had not seen him on TV in a long time, and with his white beard I almost didn't recognize him. He gave me a big bear hug and said he was glad to have me back. He asked, "Who is that sheriff of that county where you live down there in Mississippi?"

"Sheriff Walker," I answered.

"I saw him on TV," Charlie continued. "When they asked him how you survived that situation, he said, 'He's nothing but a country boy.'"

I was impressed that Charlie Daniels remembered seeing the sheriff of my county on a 30-second clip and knew who I was.

Kellie, Uncle Jerry, and Lewis Bailey arrived midmorning Wednesday. Kellie and I embraced and kissed. We are just simple country folks. There weren't fireworks flying and we didn't run through any fields in slow motion. In our own quiet way we celebrated our reunion. I was sure glad to see her and to know she was all right. I knew she went through a lot while I was in captivity.

I issued another statement on May 5 from Landstuhl, Germany, after my reunion with Kellie:

"Good morning to everyone in America, my hometown, and the rest of the world. My treatment is going very well, and I'm thankful to the outstanding medical community here in Landstuhl for their care. My recovery is definitely improving now that my wife, Kellie, is here with me.

"My only plan now is to go home as soon as possible and spend some quality, private time with my family. We trust that you will respect our wishes for privacy so we may spend this very special time together.

"All of us have prayed a lot over the last few weeks. Thank you, again, for all of your thoughts and concern for me and my family. I can only hope that the same amount of hope and effort are continued for the safety of others and for peace.

"Also, please continue to pray for all the civilians, soldiers, hostages, and my friends and colleagues who are still missing as well as their families who are going through this difficult time. My family and I will continue to keep everyone in our thoughts and prayers.

"We can't say "Thank You" enough to our family, friends, and neighbors in Macon and around the world for your never-ending support for us. And a special thank you, also, to Halliburton for going above and beyond anything we could have ever imagined to get Kellie to me as quickly as possible. Kellie brought me my favorite boots, jeans, and a red shirt so I could feel a lot more comfortable and closer to home. I'm ready to get there and hug my children."

The flight back home was great. We returned on the Halliburton jet that had flown Kellie to Germany. It was relaxing. Although it did not bother me then to talk about my experiences while held in Iraq, no one really asked. Kellie was just glad I was safe and heading home, which was good enough for her.

When we landed in Columbus, Mississippi, the media were there waiting. I was not ready for all of the attention; I didn't want anybody there. We diverted them and were escorted home by the Mississippi Highway Patrol. Colonel Harvey had warned, "You are not going to be able to go back and crawl into a hole. You are going to find that people want to 'touch the stone,' and right now you are the stone. They are going to want to be around you and associate with you. This is a big story to the media, and they are going to want it. They are going to want the exclusive. They may even fight over the story, and you are going to have to deal with it."

I told Kellie, "Now I am under more pressure and stress than when I was over there as a hostage. I can't even speak in front of a small group of people let alone millions." I just wanted to go home, let things heal, go back to Iraq, and finish my job, and then go back to driving a truck and working my farm just like it had been before. I wanted to run and hide.

Then I read in the Bible in the book of James, which states that if a man knows to do right, but doesn't do it, that it's a sin. And it'd be a sin for me not to tell people what God has done for me. I have a message and, considering the circumstances in the world and where my story took place, a wonderful opportunity to deliver it and to touch many people. There are so many folks who are not being touched. God works through us; He is now working through me to get His message out.

I am not a minister, but I saw the first time I stood in front of that courthouse the effect my story has on people.

I wasn't even planning to talk that day on the steps of the courthouse. In fact, I had told everybody that I would NOT be saying anything. I caught everyone off guard when I said that I was going to make a statement. It hit me right then that I needed to talk, and I just started talking. I said, "I want to thank everybody for their prayers and support. I knew I was going to make it. I knew I was coming home. He'd given me a peace the whole time. And I told the Lord to pick the time and place. And when he gave me an opportunity, I said, 'Lord, if today is my day you call me home, so be it. If it's not, then I am going to these guys and I am going home.' They made no bones about what they would do if I tried to escape. I was a captive. I was not there of my free will. I couldn't leave when I wanted to unless I escaped."

I was nervous, but it felt good to thank the people who'd been praying for my family and to tell the story of how God protected me. Still, I just wanted to get back to some normalcy.

I plan to continue to speak to groups and get the good news, the message, that is within my story. The people who hear me are letting me know which parts of the story are more inspirational and which parts are the most interesting.

I was overwhelmed by the magnitude my story had reached. We have received upwards of 1,500 letters and more phone calls than we can count. Letters have come from all over the world, places such as, England, Australia, Poland, Canada, and many other countries. I didn't realize just how much the fascination with my story had grown.

FOR IMMEDIATE RELEASE:

May 8, 2004 HALLIBURTON AND THOMAS HAMILL

Halliburton and Thomas Hamill issued the following statement upon his return to his hometown of Macon, Miss., on May 8. "It is with extreme pleasure that Halliburton is the first to welcome Tommy home to the United States and, more importantly, to return him to his family in Macon, Miss. During his treatment in Germany, Tommy's recovery was expedited with the arrival early-on of his wife, Kellie. Tommy is grateful to Halliburton and the medical staff in Landstuhl for ensuring his treatment was exceptional as well as private. 'This is more than I ever would have imagined,' said Hamill, as he privately celebrated his 44th birthday on Thursday with a small group including his wife, Halliburton personnel and several soldiers. 'I'd do anything possible to thank the company for everything they've done for me and my family and to keep supporting the troops. I continue to pray for my two missing colleagues, the safety of my friends and co-workers in Iraq as well as the families of those who have lost a loved one.' When presented with mementos from the company and the military prior to his departure from Germany, Hamill was hailed as 'someone who epitomizes the definition of a true American hero.'

Upon his arrival in Mississippi, Hamill stated he was thankful to Halliburton for the return trip home and very happy to be on American soil again. His first priority will be to spend private time with his family and continue his medical treatment. We urge you to respect the family's request for privacy during this emotional time."

The Halliburton people asked my family to come to Houston, Texas, to meet with company executives. The Houston Astros team wanted me to throw out the ceremonial first pitch of a game they were playing against the Florida Marlins on Wednesday night May 12th. I have always loved baseball and was pleased to have been asked, but my son Thomas threw out the first pitch and I threw out the second.

FOR IMMEDIATE RELEASE:
May 12, 2004 HALLIBURTON AND THOMAS HAMILL
Halliburton and Thomas Hamill issued the following statement during his visit to Halliburton's hometown of Houston on May 12.

"It is with extreme honor that Halliburton welcomes Tommy and his family to Houston. Halliburton is thrilled to host Tommy and his wife, Kellie; son, Thomas; and daughter, Tori.

'Tommy epitomizes the definition of a true American hero and the humble spirit of a Halliburton employee and we're proud he's part of our family,' explained Halliburton President and Chief Executive Officer Dave Lesar. 'Tommy held his faith and composure bravely and relentlessly. He never lost hope and neither did Halliburton.'

During their visit to Houston, Tommy and his family will meet their many supportive friends and co-workers within Halliburton and the Hamills will throw out the ceremonial first pitch at the Houston Astros-Florida Marlins game at Minute Maid Park on May 12 as part of Heroes Week at the ballpark.

'This is more than I ever would have imagined,' said Hamill, as he met privately with Lesar at the company's headquarters.

There's no way I can thank Halliburton enough for everything they've done for my family and me and to keep supporting the troops. Halliburton's support has been above and beyond anything I ever thought possible by a company this big and I thank them wholeheartedly,' said Hamill. 'The company has embraced me and my family and we're proud to be part of such a wonderful group of people.'"

The week following my return from Houston to Macon, Doctors Scott Jones and Charles Rhea of Columbus examined my wounded right arm. They set a plan for two surgeries.

First, they did a skin graft at the end of that week. A strip of skin roughly an inch and a half wide and five inches long was cut from the top of my right thigh and placed on the wound. My leg hurt more than my arm the next day, but the graft did very well.

The second surgery was done to insert a thin titanium rod through the ulna bone in my right forearm. An incision starting about two inches in from my elbow and running to within two inches of my wrist was needed to insert the rod. At my last appointment with Doctor Rhea in September he was amazed at how well the bone was healing, but I may face bone-graft surgery in the future.

During my recovery at home I thought and prayed for

six weeks before I decided to publish this book. I have heard from so many people who want to hear the whole story, which has helped me realize I do indeed have a message of how faith can conquer evil and how the power of prayer can work in the most difficult circumstances.

Many people try to fill a void they have in their lives by "touching the stone." Individuals who are compelled to meet face to face often approach survivors, like me, often traveling great distances for a chance encounter. I have experienced this phenomenon on several occasions and found it rather difficult to understand. I've had people show up at my house who have driven for days having no idea I would even be home. This is my opportunity, in this book, to tell the world that I'm just a messenger of the fact that God is at work in our lives. It's my hope that the telling of my story will lead people to "touch the cross" of Christ instead.

*Tommy makes his first public appearance in Germany
at the Landstuhl Regional Medical Center.*

*Kellie and Uncle Jerry board a Halliburton jet headed
for Germany to bring Tommy home.*

*Mark Lee, Colonel Harvey, Kellie, Tommy, and Jason
stand outside the Fisher House in Germany. The Fisher House
provides a home for families visiting loved ones
in the Landstuhl Regional Medical Center.*

From left to right: Tommy, Uncle Jerry, and Mark Lee
relax in Germany after Tommy's escape.

*Members of the media surround Tommy after his address
on July 3, in Macon, Mississippi.*

*Tommy and Kellie embrace on the steps of the
Noxubee County courthouse at the first prayer vigil since
Tommy's escape. Tommy's father, Leo Hamill,
stands in the background.*

*Tori Hamill's Eighth-grade class made this sign
to welcome Tommy home.*

*Tommy addressed students at the High School in Sachse, Texas,
where Kellie's father, Wallace Green, works.*

*Tommy appeared on the cover of Progressive
Farmer magazine in August 2004.*

Doris Yoder, at Tommy's left, and Jesse Green left their jobs for a month to stay with Kellie during Tommy's captivity.

Family and friends join in prayer behind the Hamill home on May 8, 2004, at a picnic celebrating Tommy's return.

*Tommy waits with his family on the pitcher's mound
at the Houston Astros game.*

Tommy and Kellie participated in the American Eagle Foundation's release of bald eagles in Tennessee on July 23, 2004. Tommy is holding an eagle named "America."

*Tommy greets young well-wisher Stephanie Kauffman
at the July 3rd parade in Macon, Mississippi.*

*A supporter welcomes Tommy home at the
July 3rd parade honoring him and local veterans.*

The Hamills have grown closer since their 24-day ordeal.

The Hamill family reunited.

*Tommy proudly displays a flag given to him by a soldier of the
2nd Battalion, 108th Infantry. The soldier had carried
the flag since he left the United States.*

Thousands of KBR employees risk
their lives everyday in distant lands to
support America's military troops.
Here we honor the memories
of the men who served in
Thomas Hamill's convoy April 9, 2004.

In Memorium

Killed in Action

Stephen Fisher; York, Nebraska
Steven Hulett; Manistee, Michigan
Tony Johnson; Riverside, California
Jack Montague; Pittsburg, Illinois
Jeffery Parker; Lake Charles, Louisiana

Missing in Action

Timothy Bell; Mobile, Alabama
William Bradley; Galveston, Texas

*L*ord, we pray for
courage, strength,
and wisdom
for our leaders,
And we ask You to
bless our nation.

ABOUT THE AUTHOR

Paul T. Brown is an award winning, and nationally acclaimed author and wildlife photographer. He was named Conservation Communicator of the Year in 1998 and 2003 for the states of Alabama and Mississippi, respectively. His work has appeared in such magazines as *Field & Stream, Outdoor Life, Sports Afield, Sporting Classics,* and many others.

Photo by Jessica Brown

Other books by Paul T. Brown are: *Conserving Wild America, Freedom Matters, Wildlife of the South, Paul Brown's Wild Visions,* and *Wild About Babies.*

For more information about Paul's books, calendars and prints, including *Praying Eagles,* go to www.trueexposures.com or call 800-323-3398.